TRACE THAT FACE

52 CUTE ANIMALS!

A Year of Cute-Induced Calm: A Tracing Book to Lift Your Mood Every Week

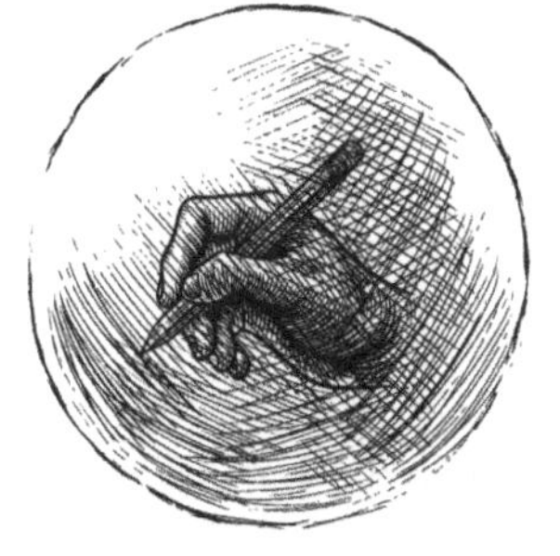

Trace & Shade Studio

INTRODUCTION

A Year of Cute-Induced Calm, One Face at a Time

Welcome to your happiest year yet!

Inside this book, you'll meet 52 of the world's most adorable creatures—puppies, kittens, bunnies, fox kits, and more—each captured in a moment of pure joy. Every face was designed to make you smile as you trace, laugh, and unwind.

This isn't a serious art project. It's a happiness habit. Trace one cute face a week —or whenever you need a pick-me-up— and watch how quickly your mood lifts. **The act of tracing slows your thoughts, focuses your breath, and invites your brain to follow the line of joy right into a grin.**

Each page is a little spark of serotonin: a giggle, a snuggle, a boop, a nap. Together, these 52 faces form a gentle, year-long rhythm of happiness and calm —no goals, no perfection, just smiles.

So grab your pen, take a deep breath, and meet your next adorable friend. Trace slowly, smile freely, and let this be your **Year of Cute-Induced Calm**.

52 weeks. 52 faces. Infinite smiles.

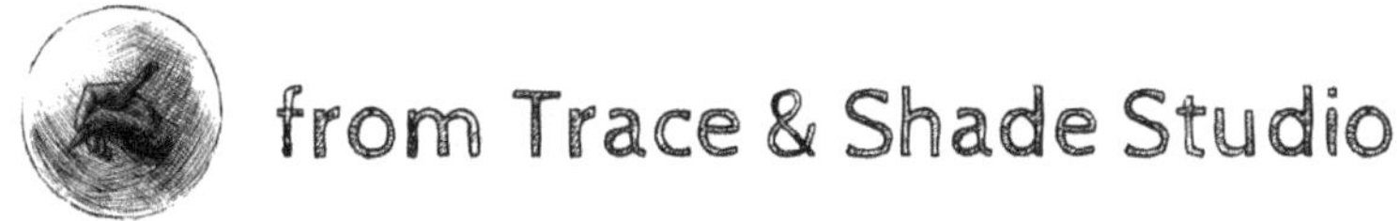

Get 10 MORE <u>FREE</u> downloadable CUTE ANIMAL FACES TO TRACE!

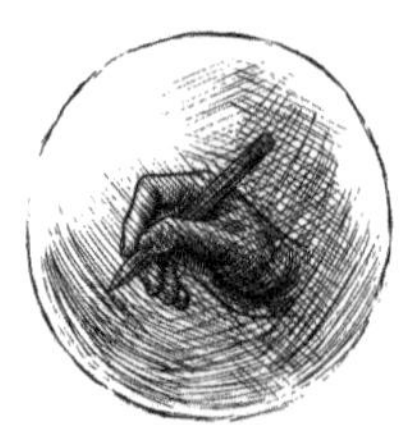

Trace
& Shade
Studio

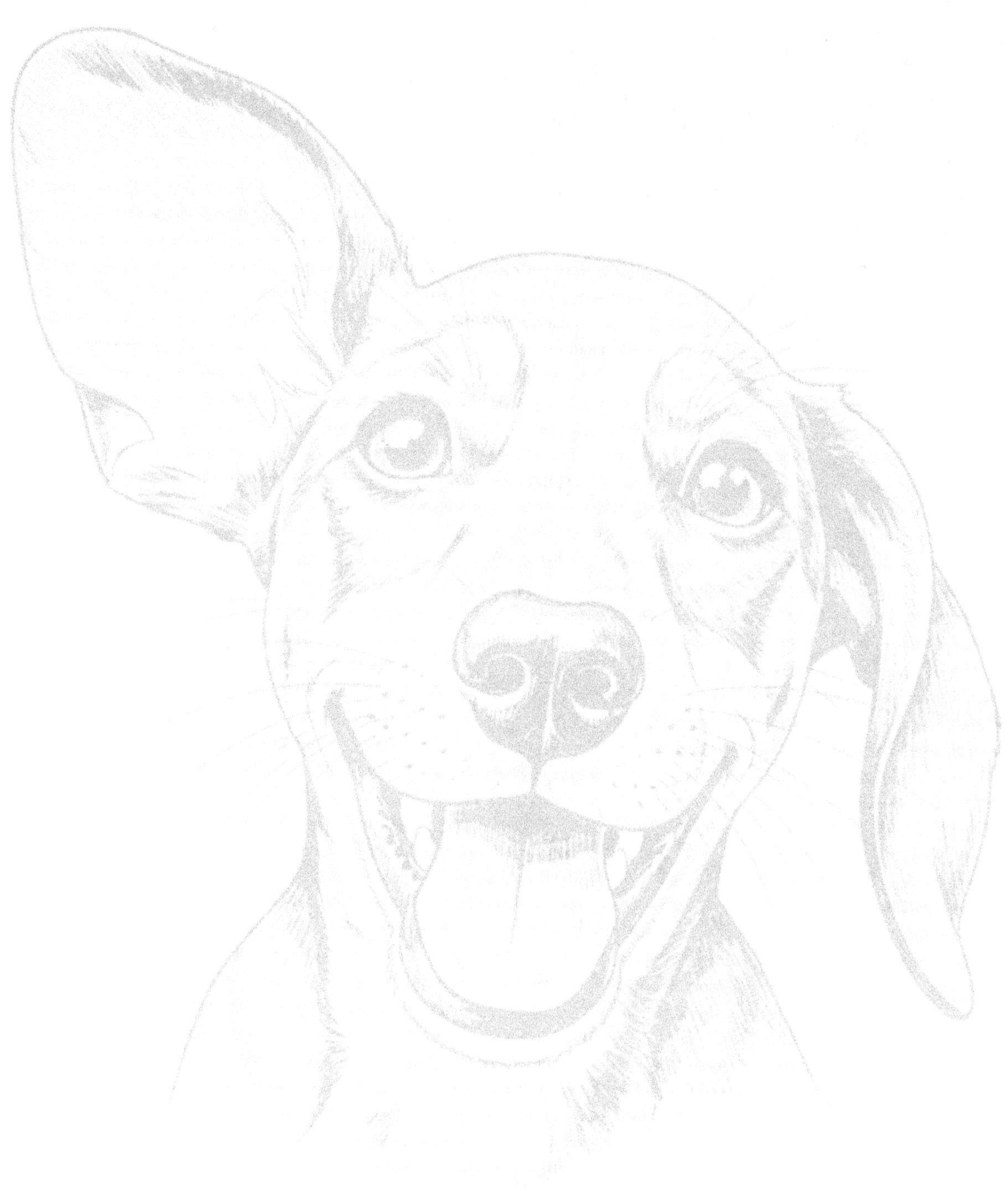

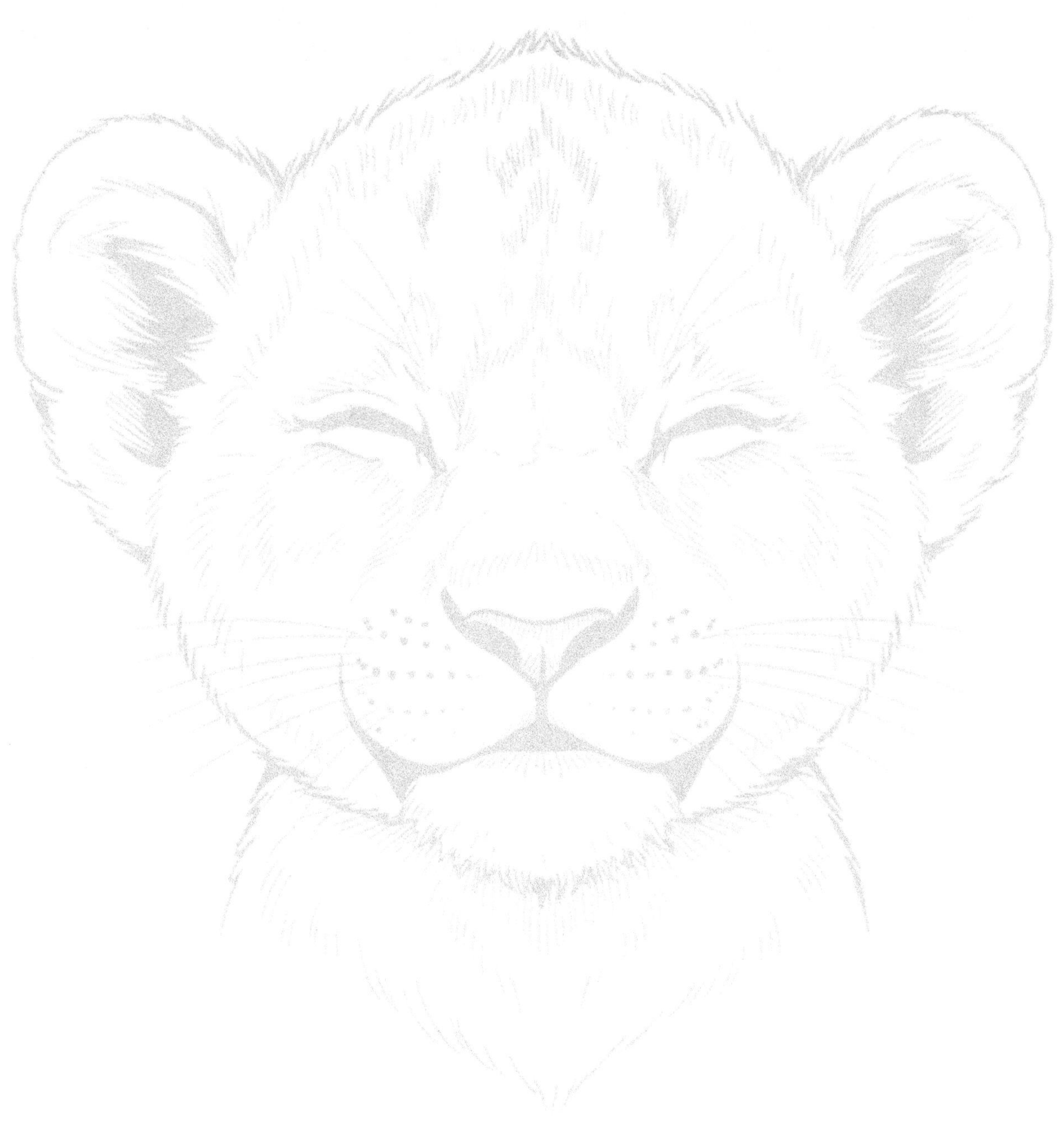

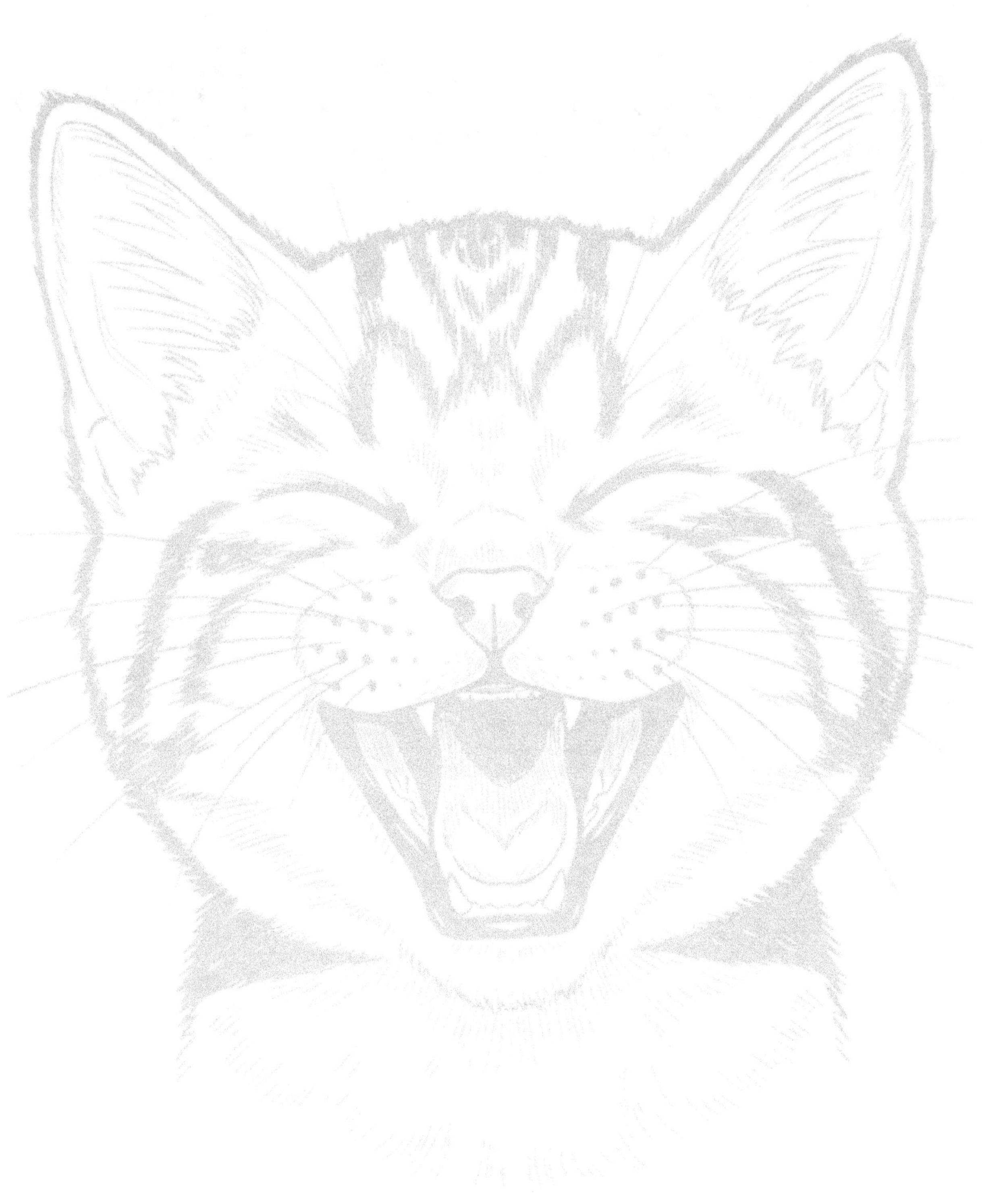

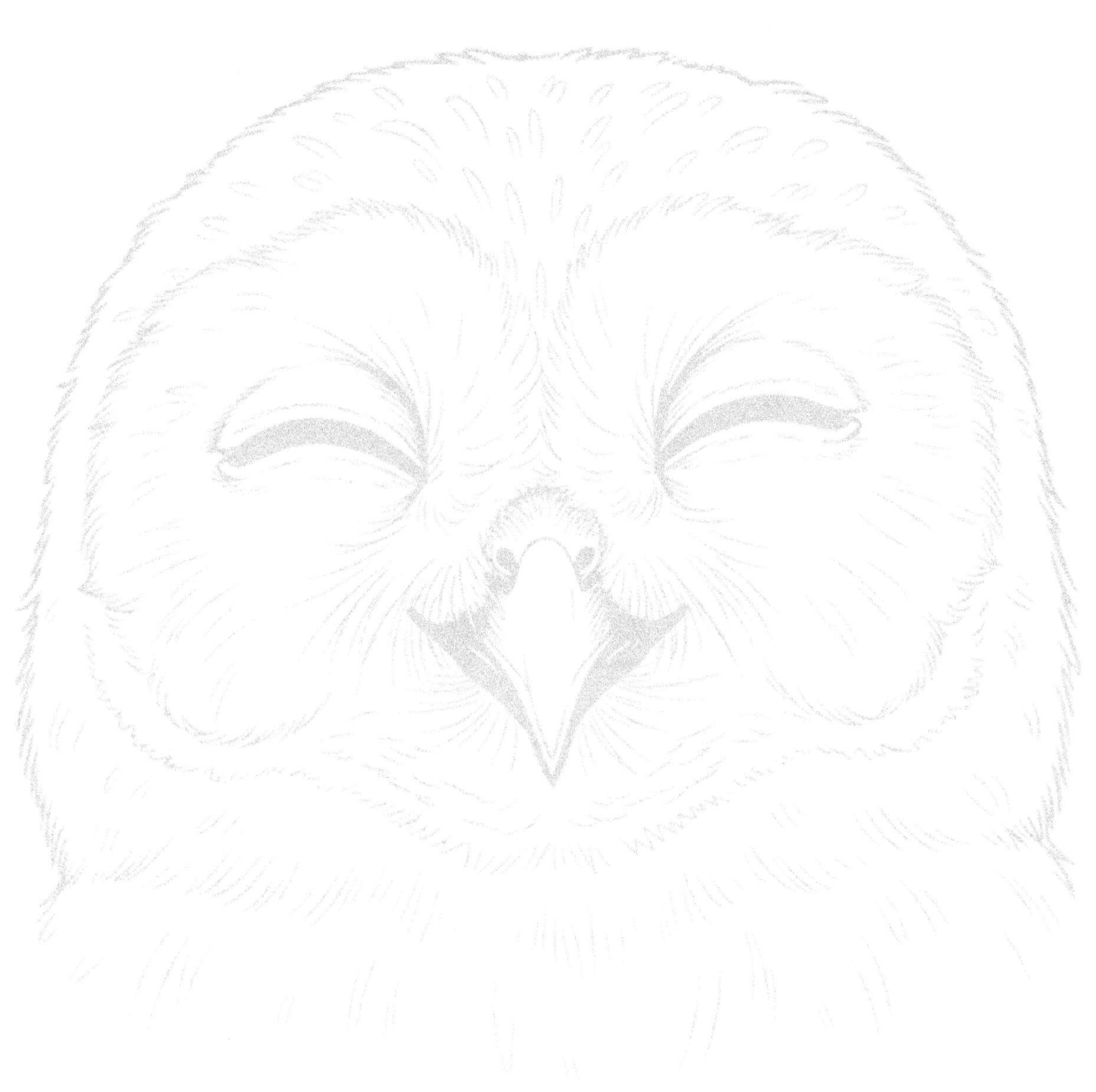

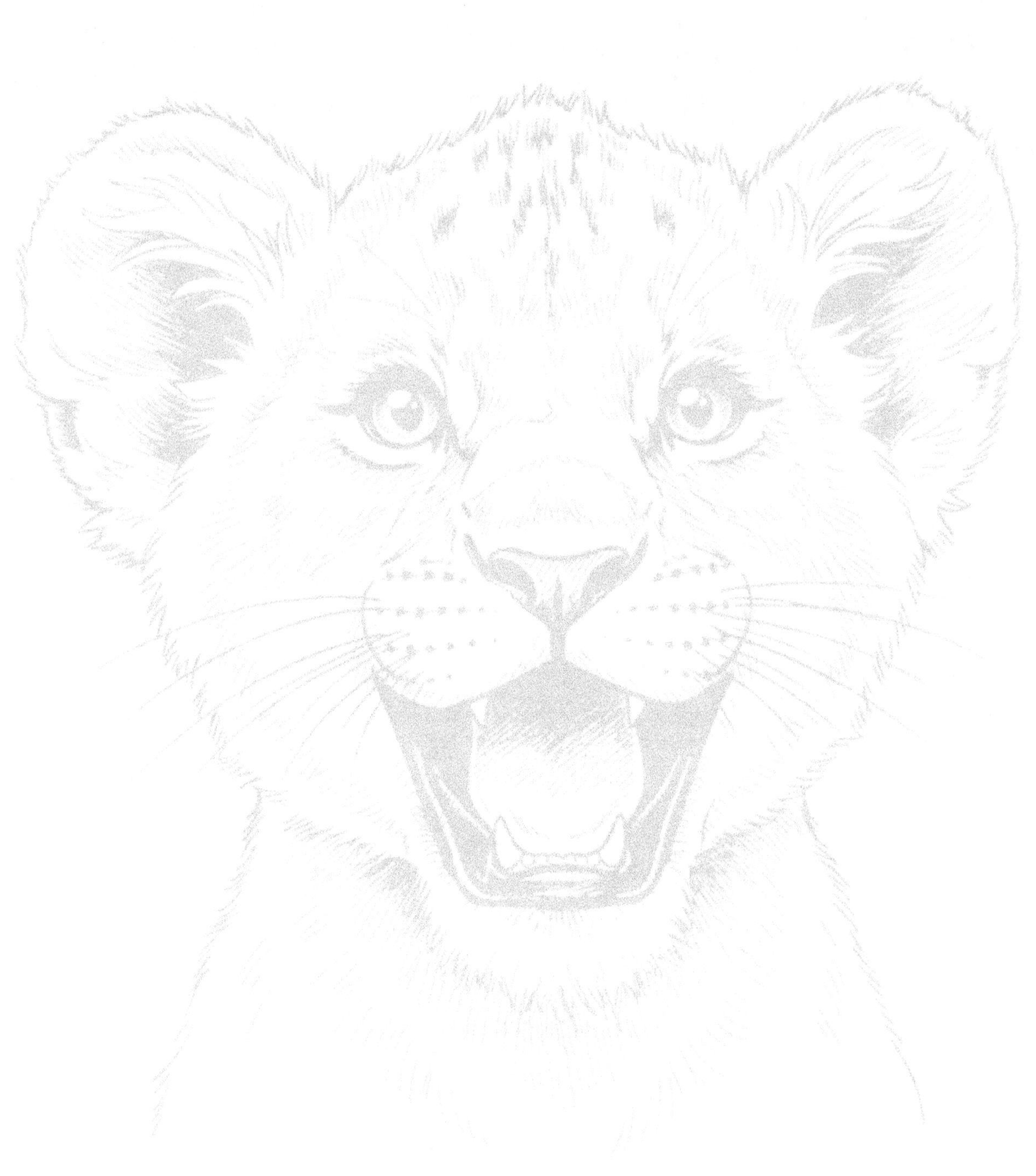

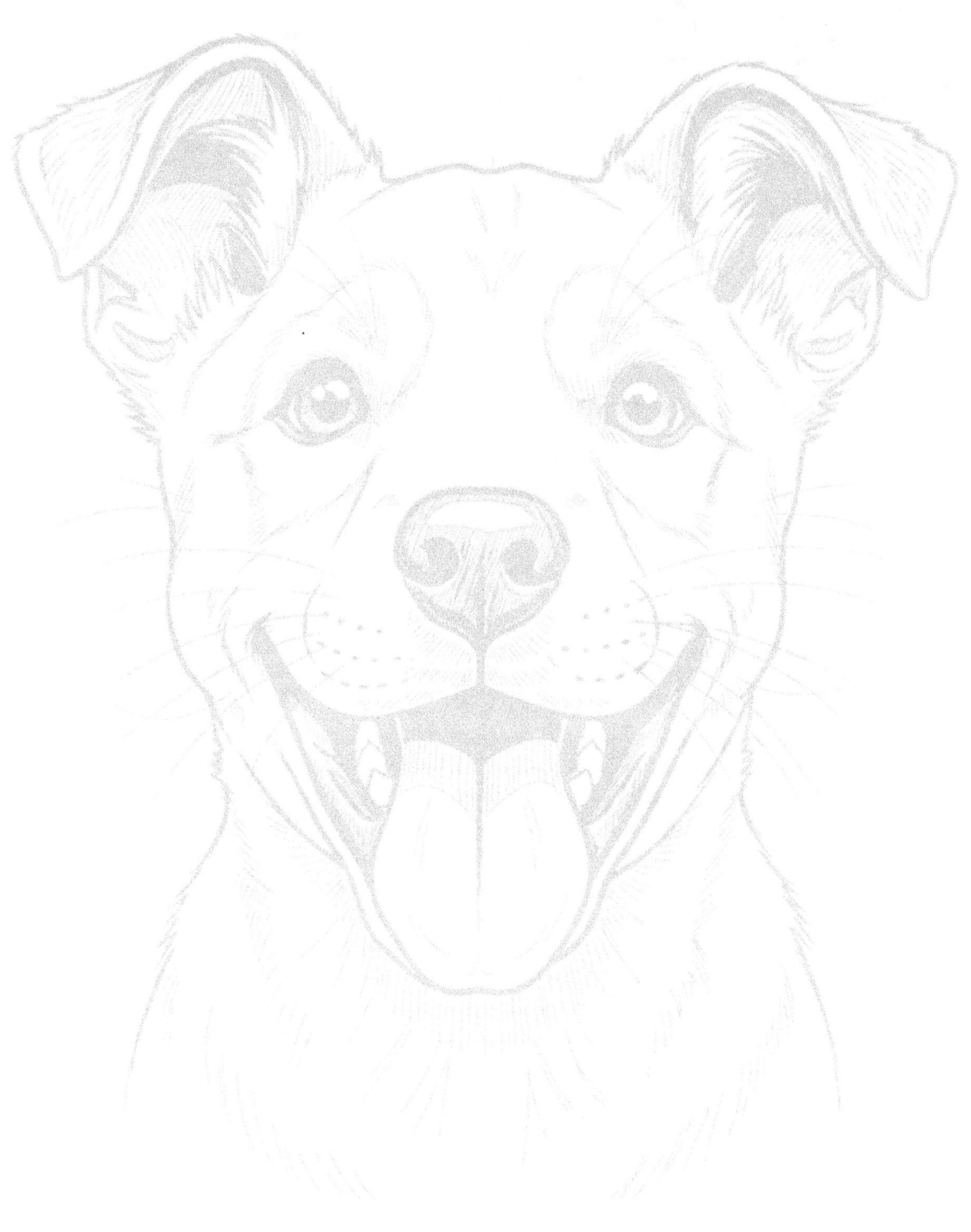

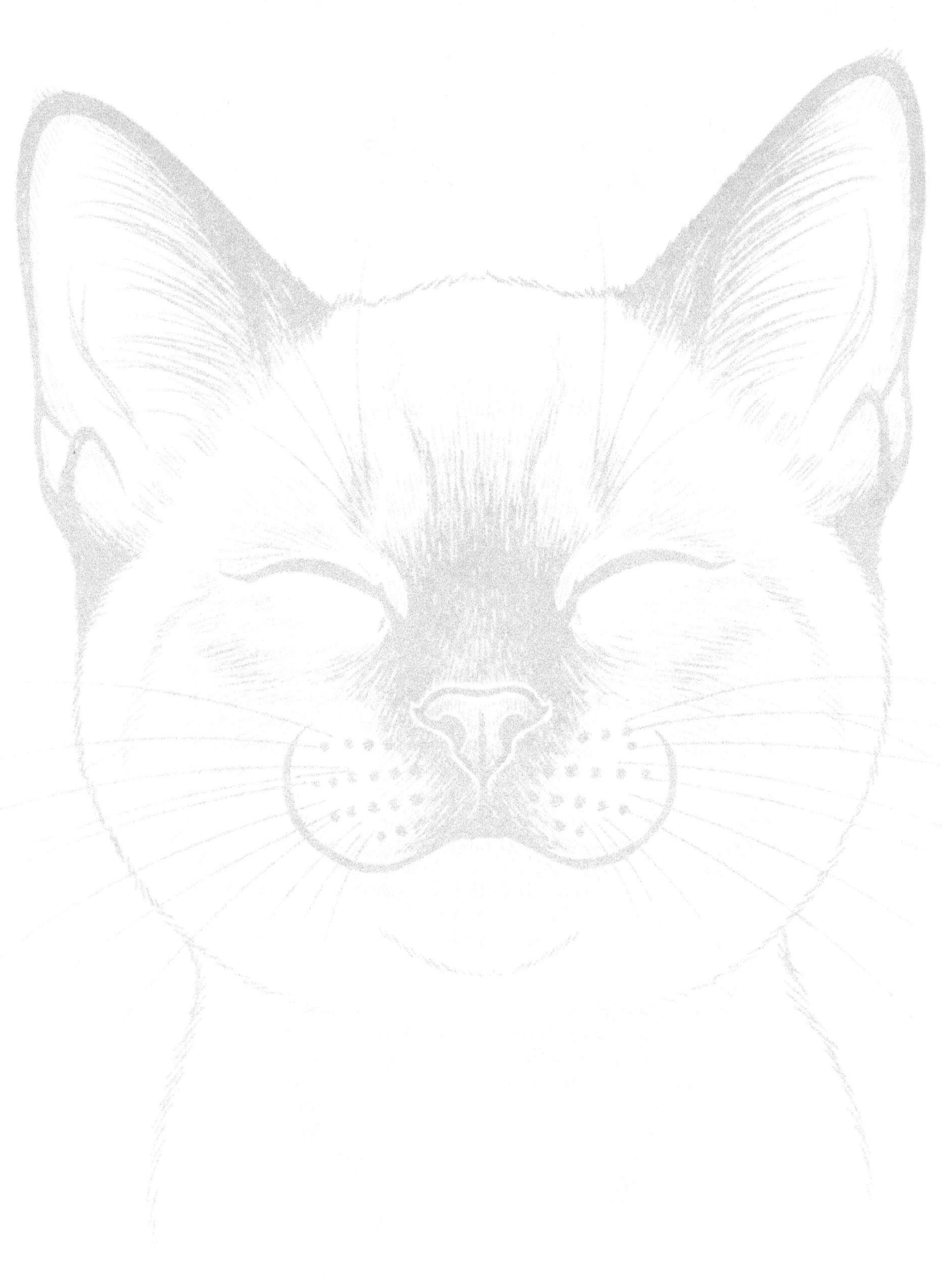

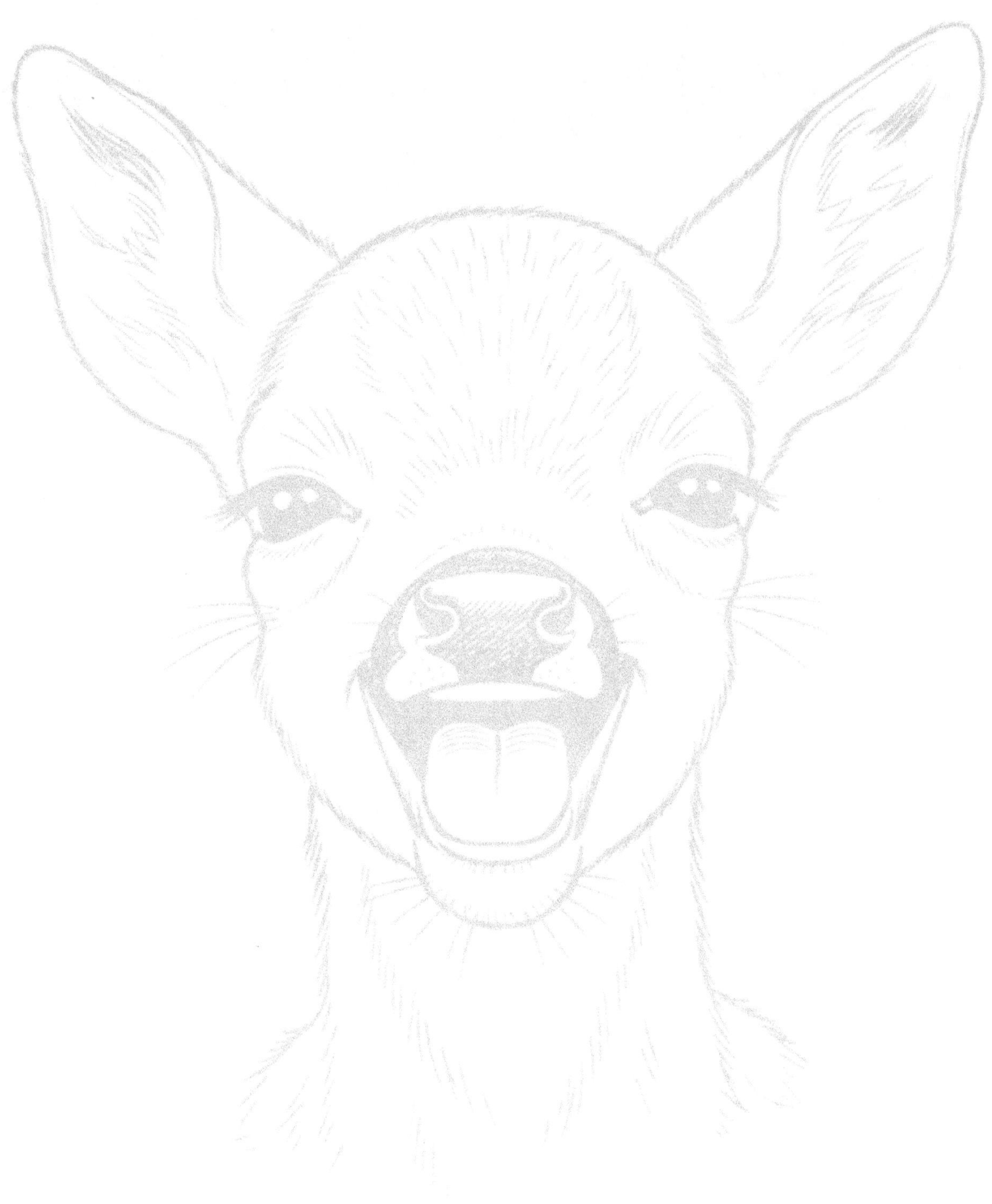

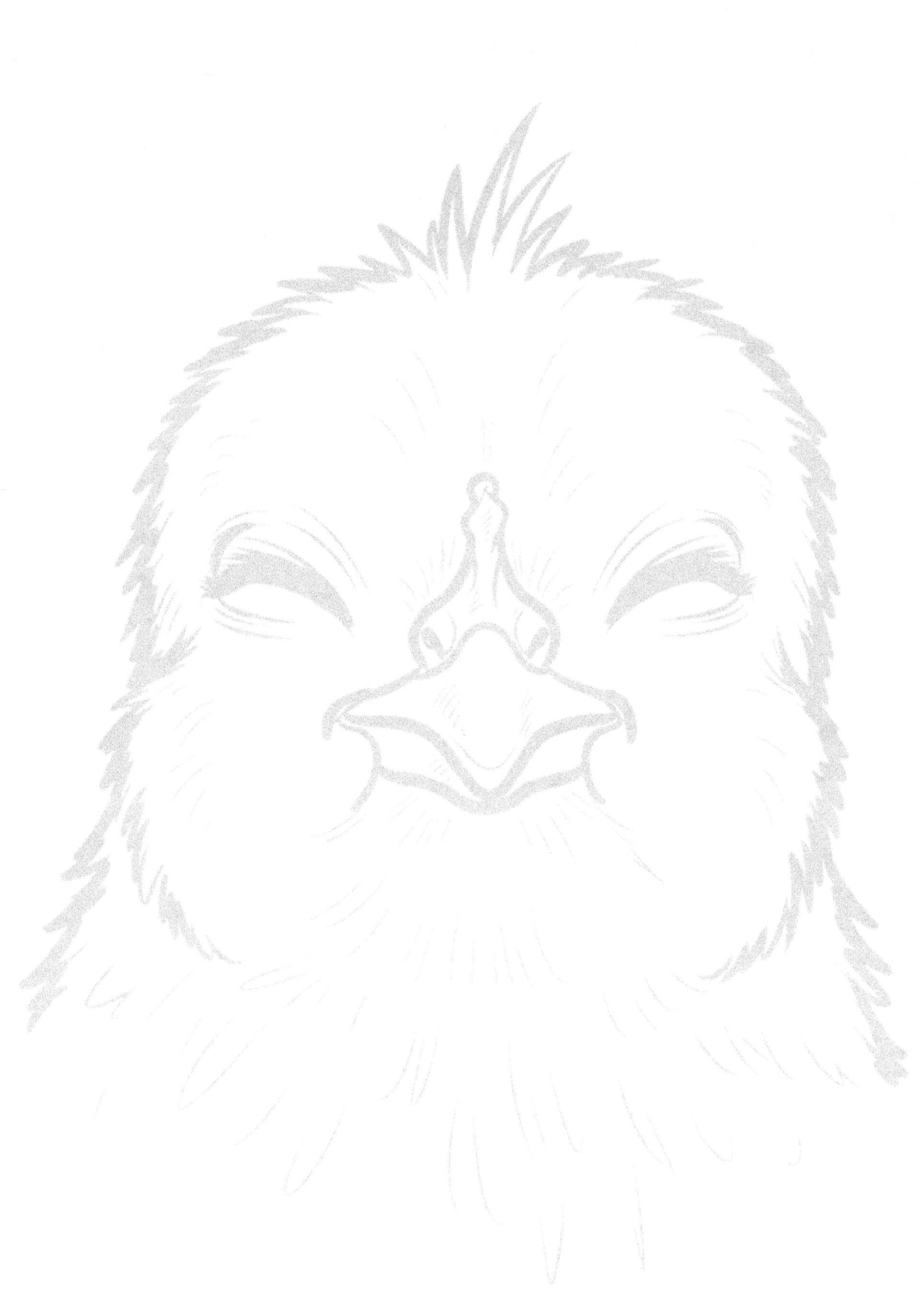

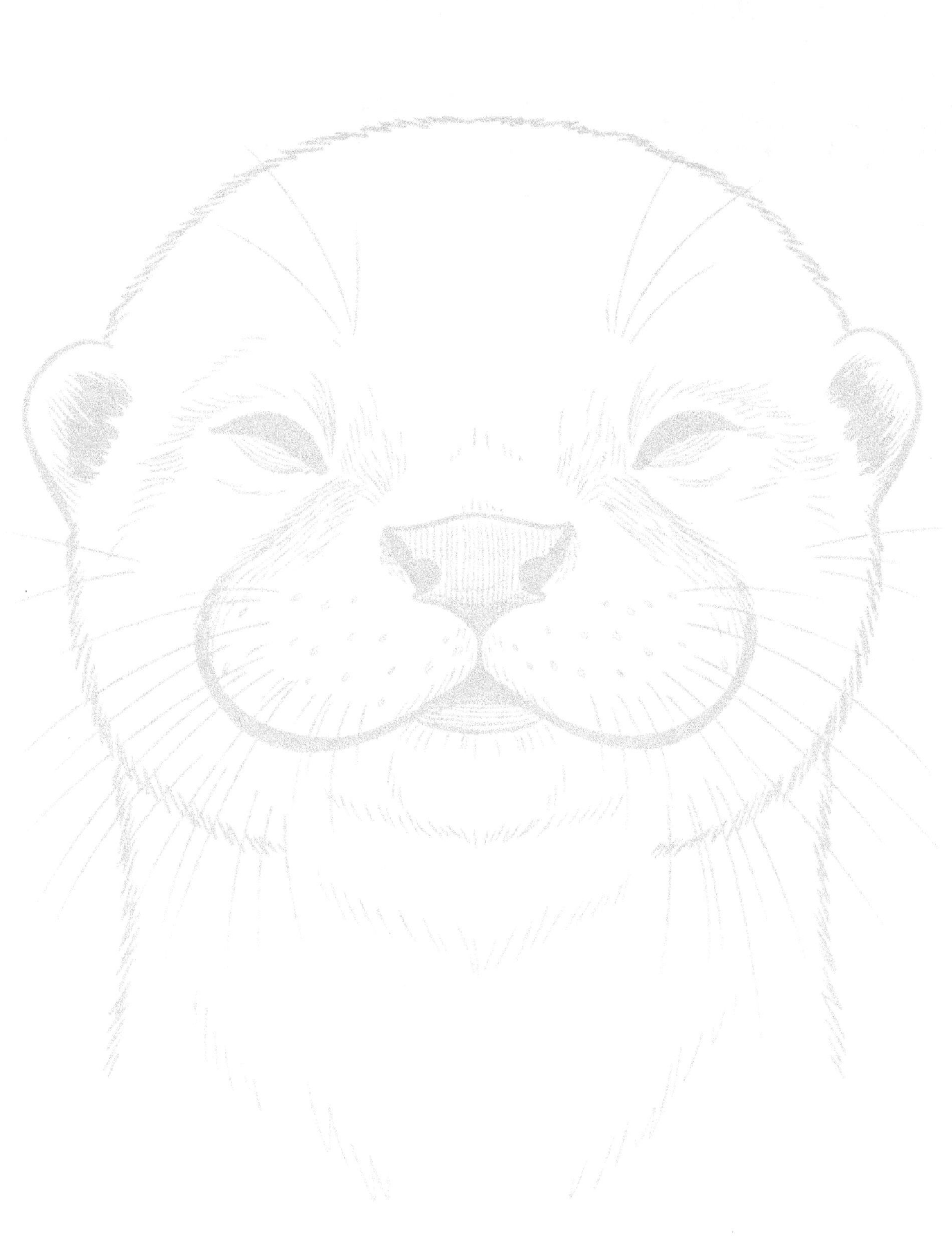

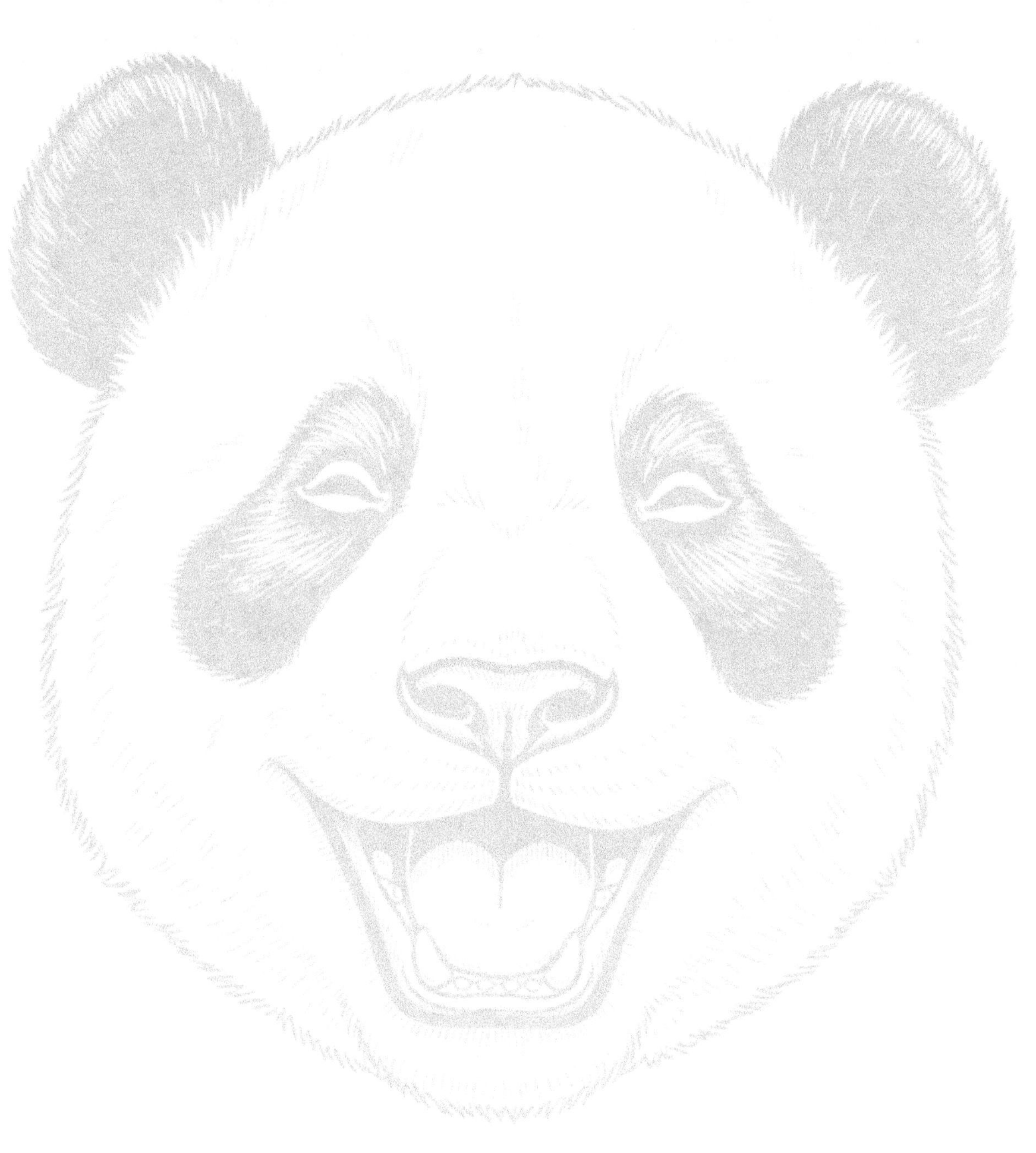

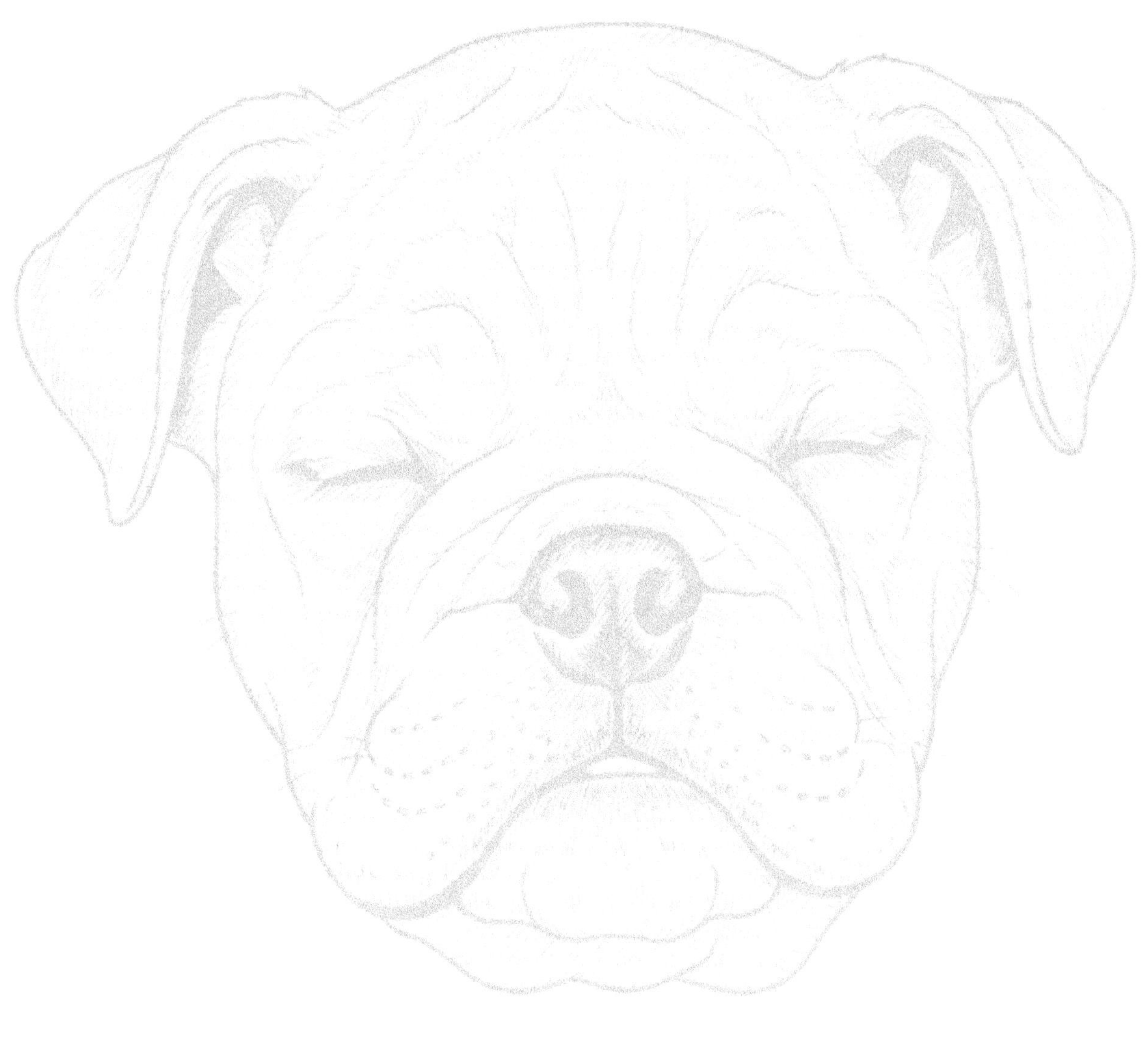

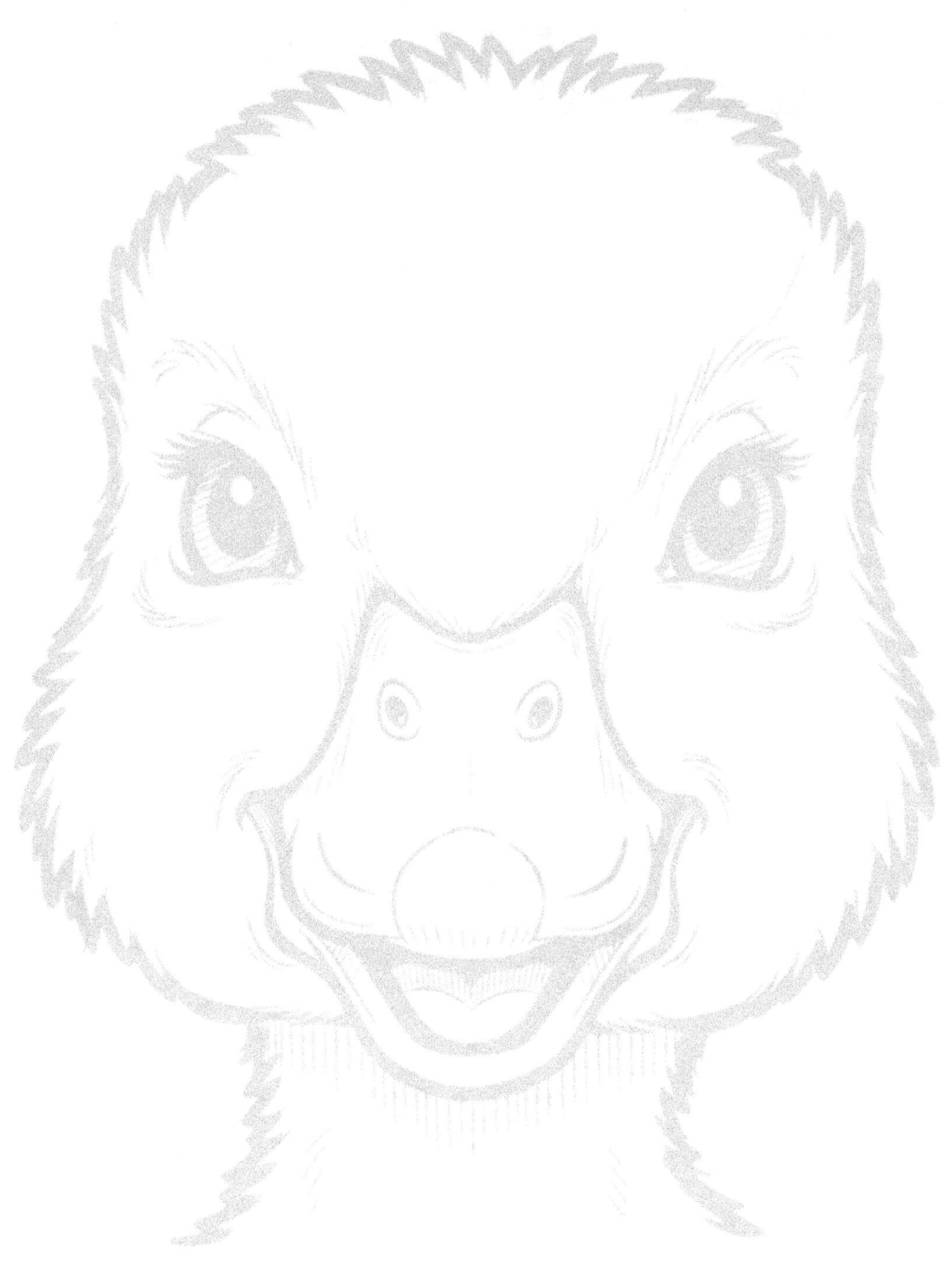

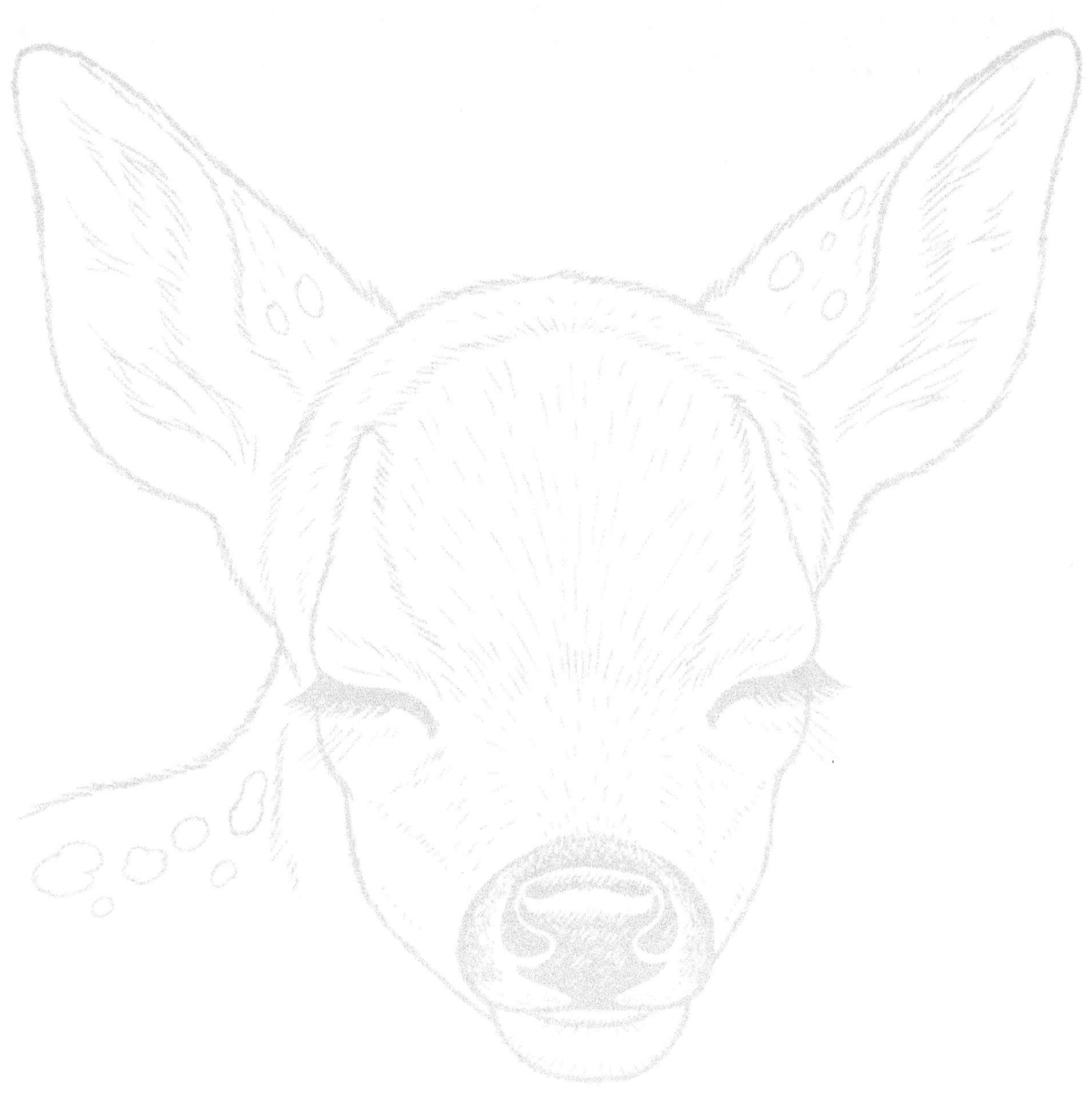

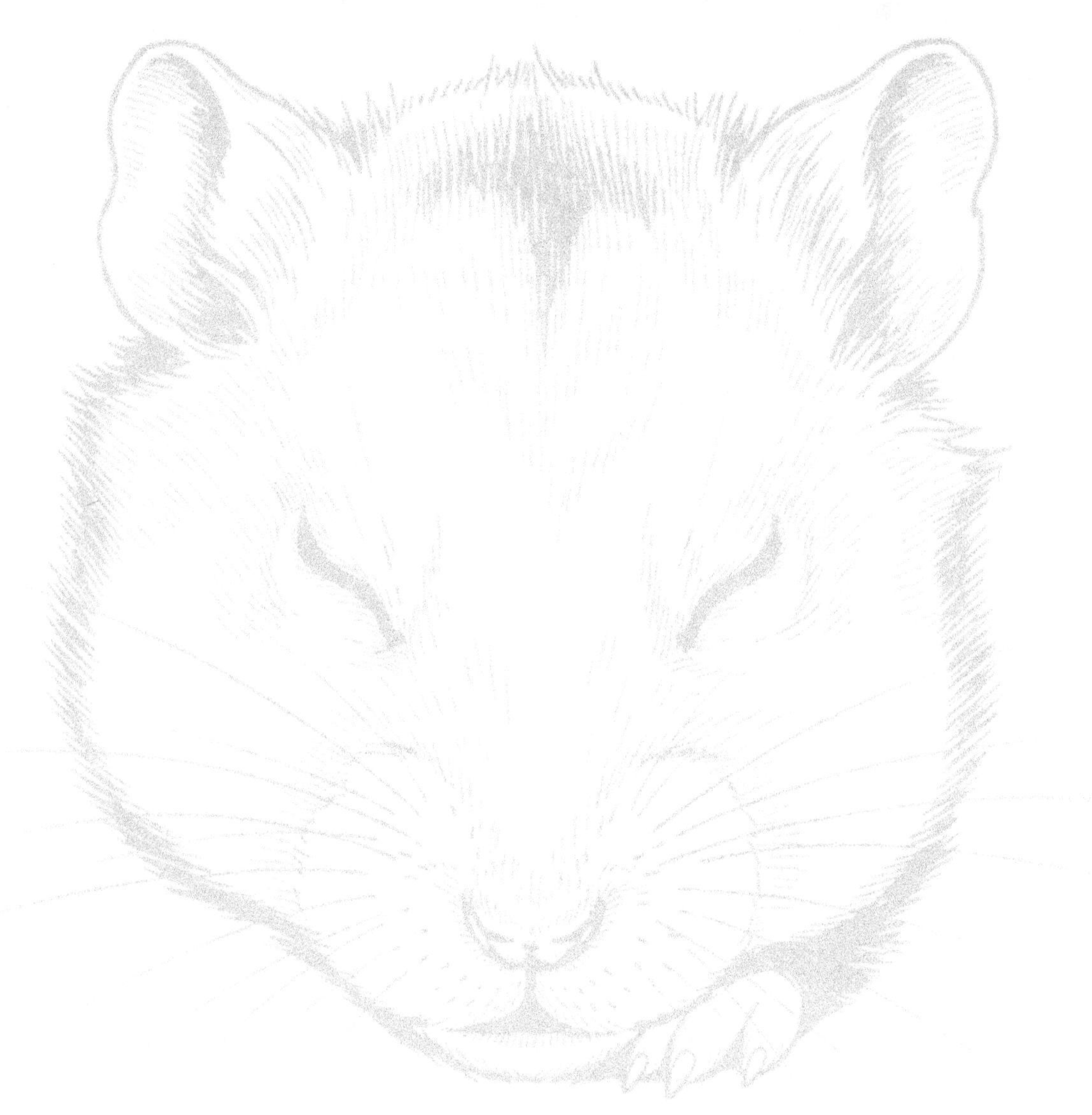

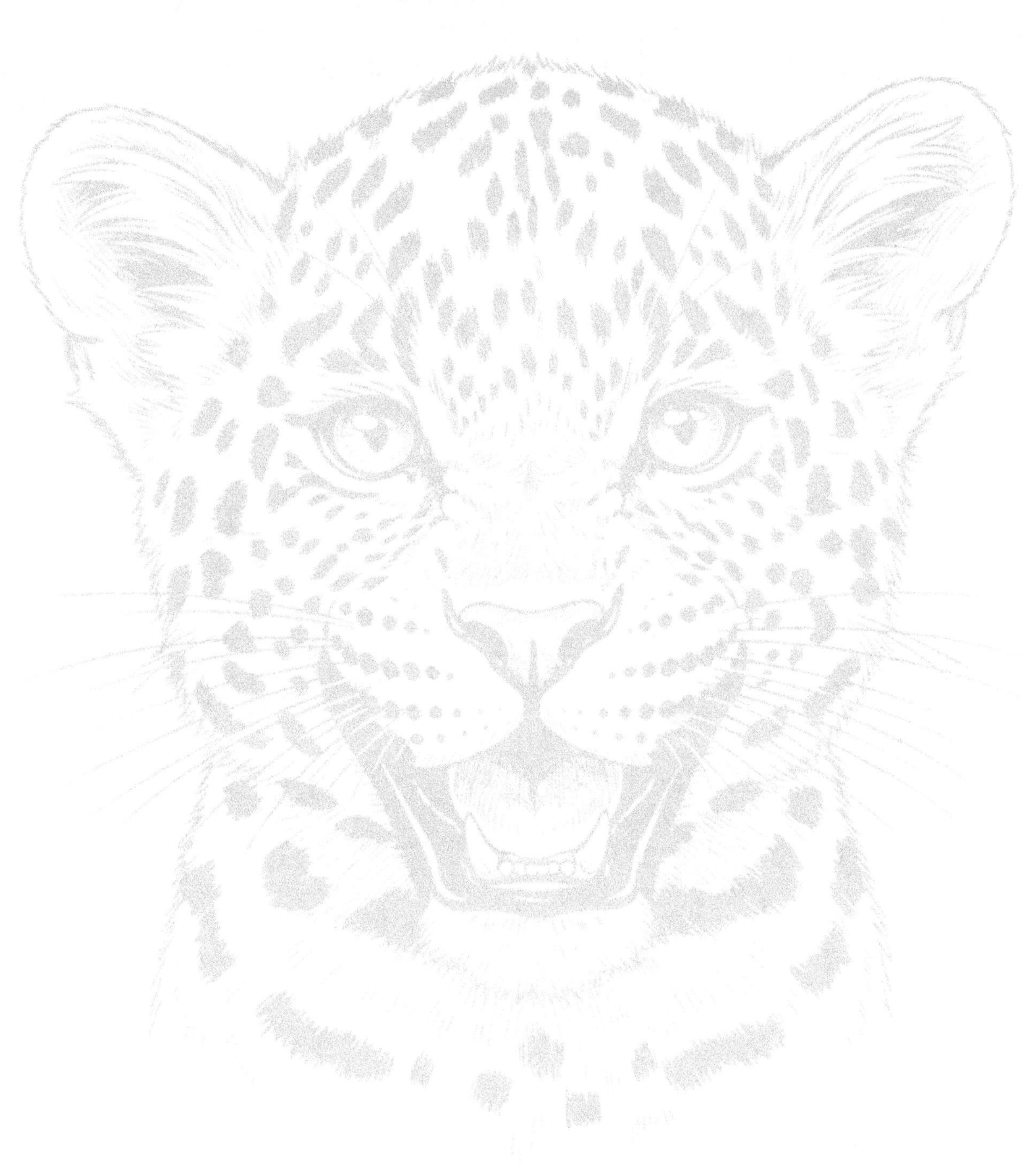

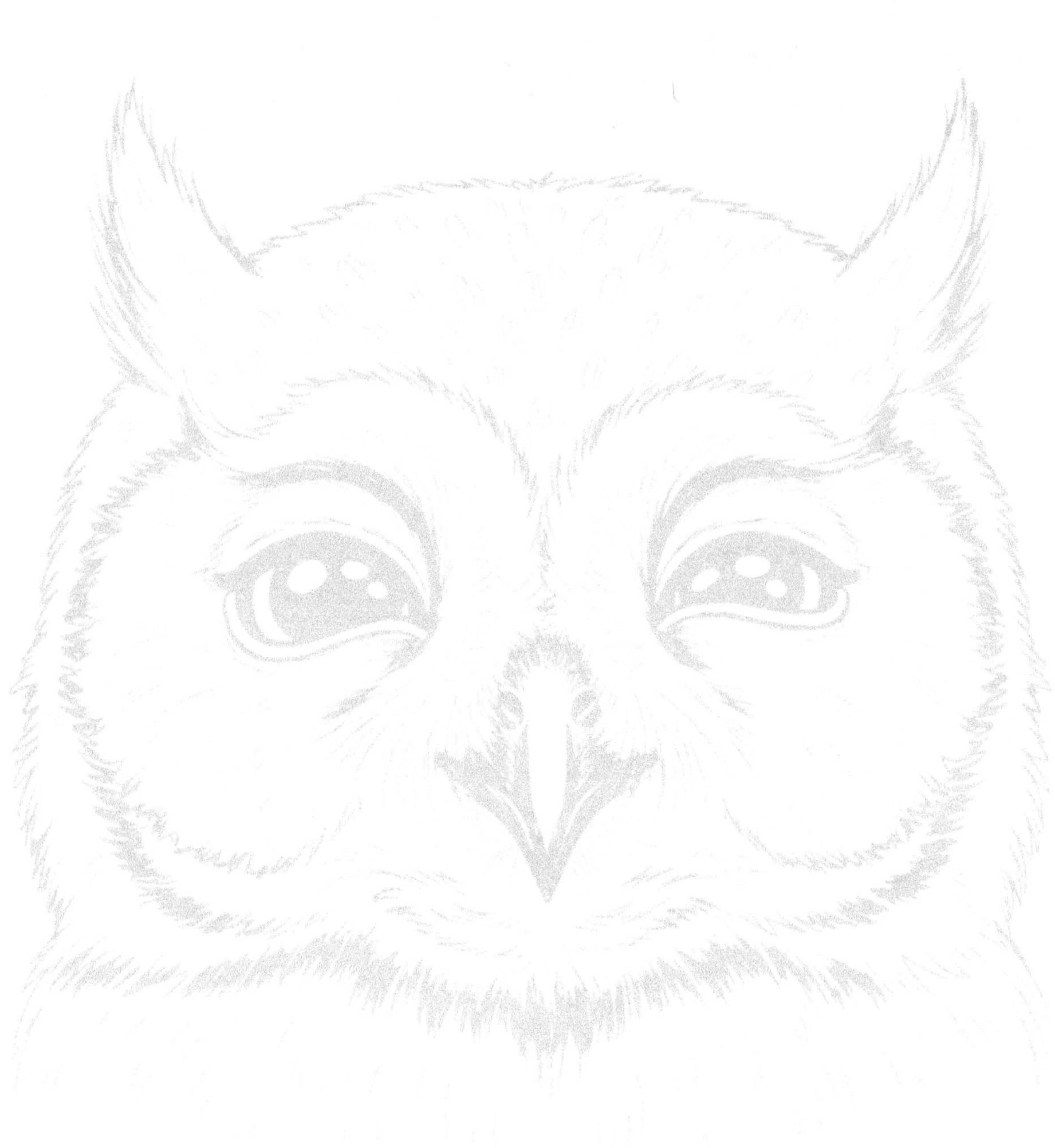

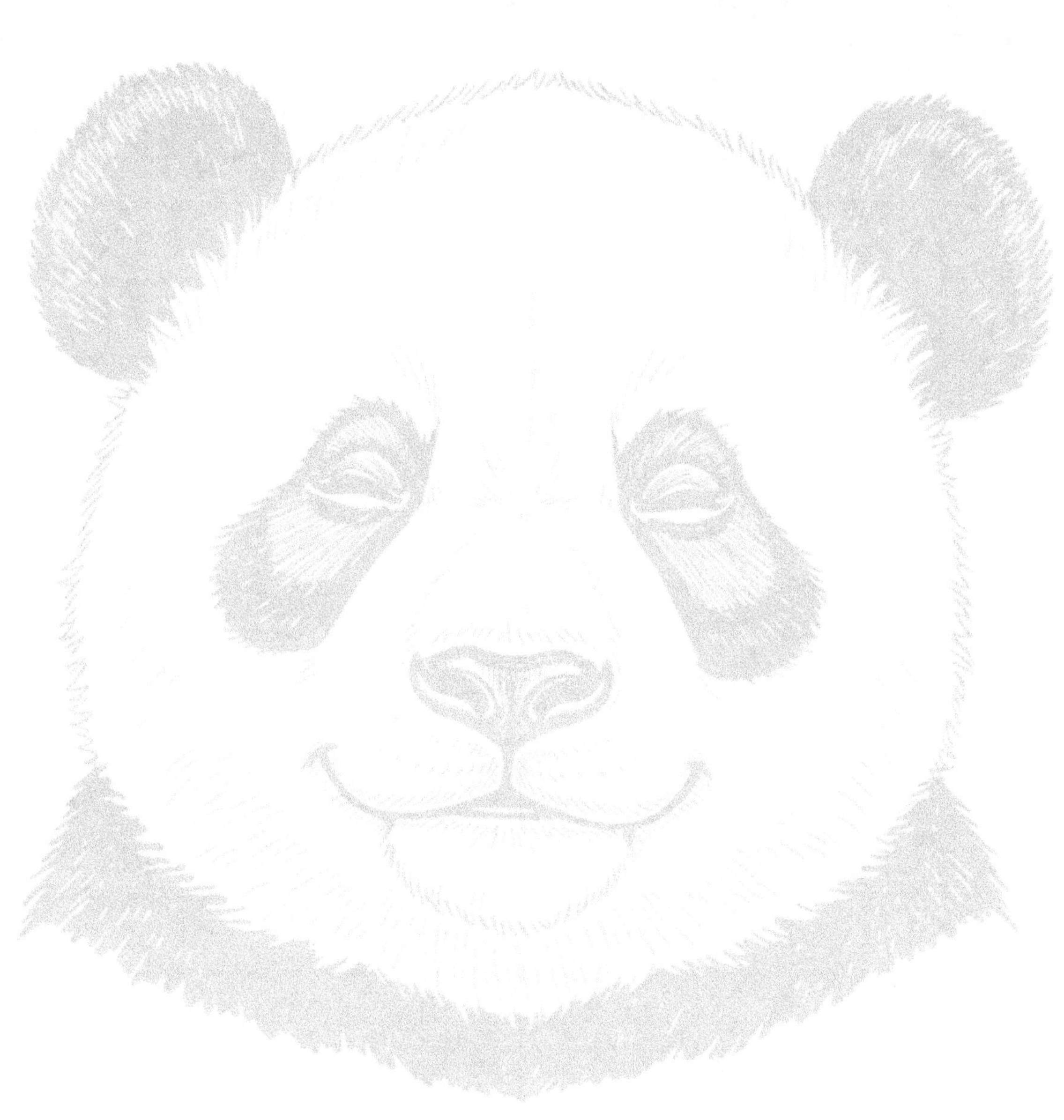

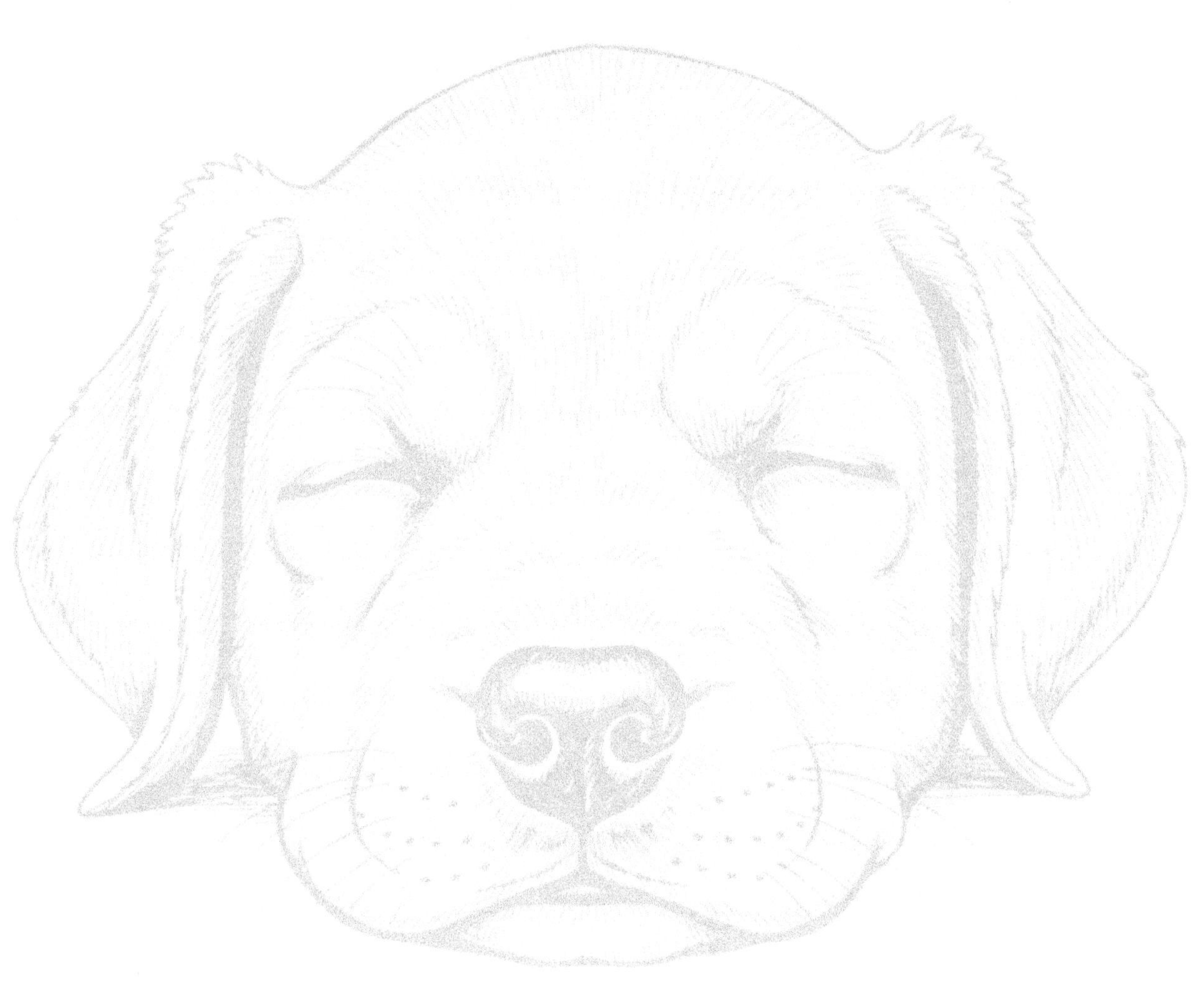

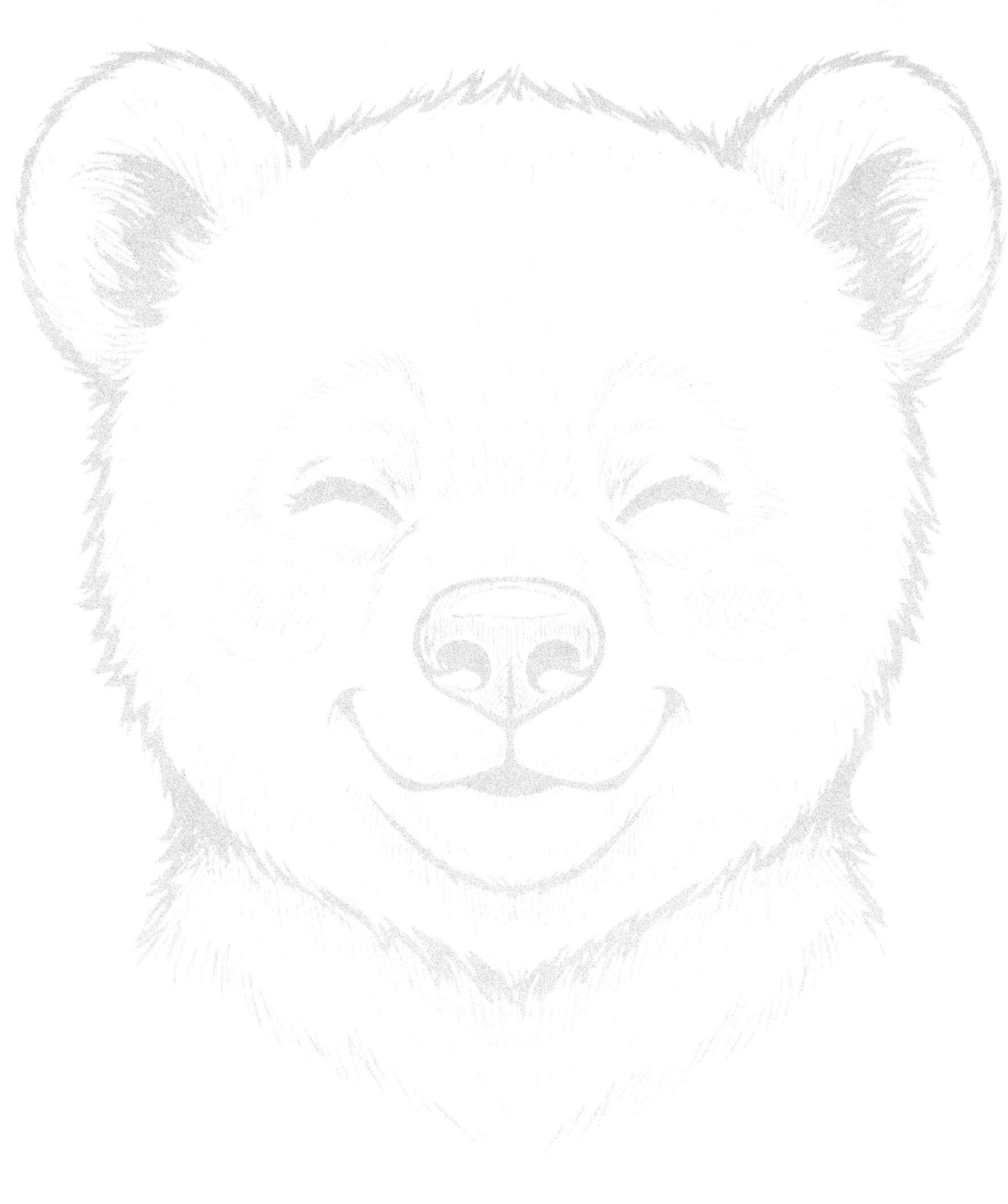

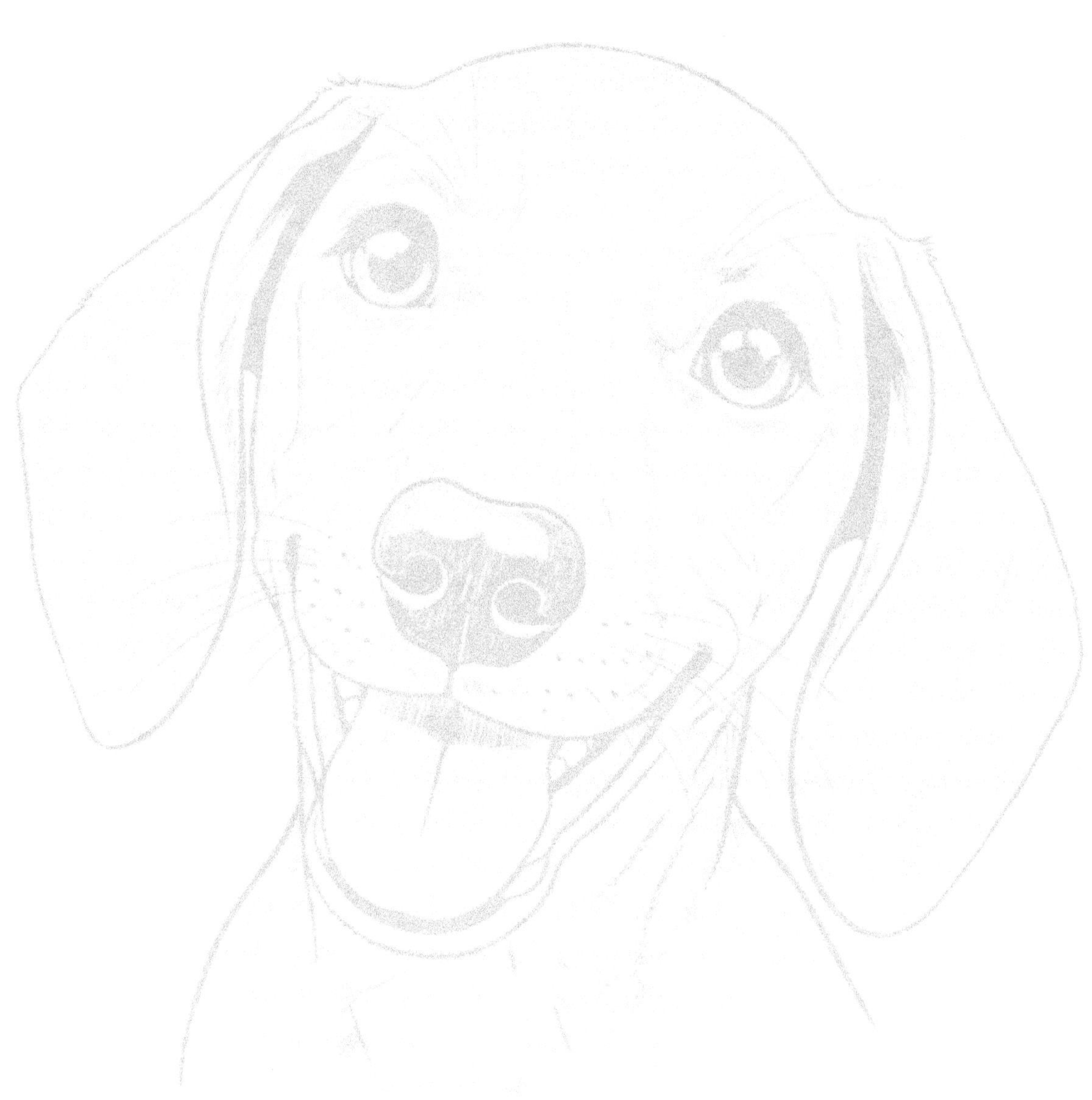

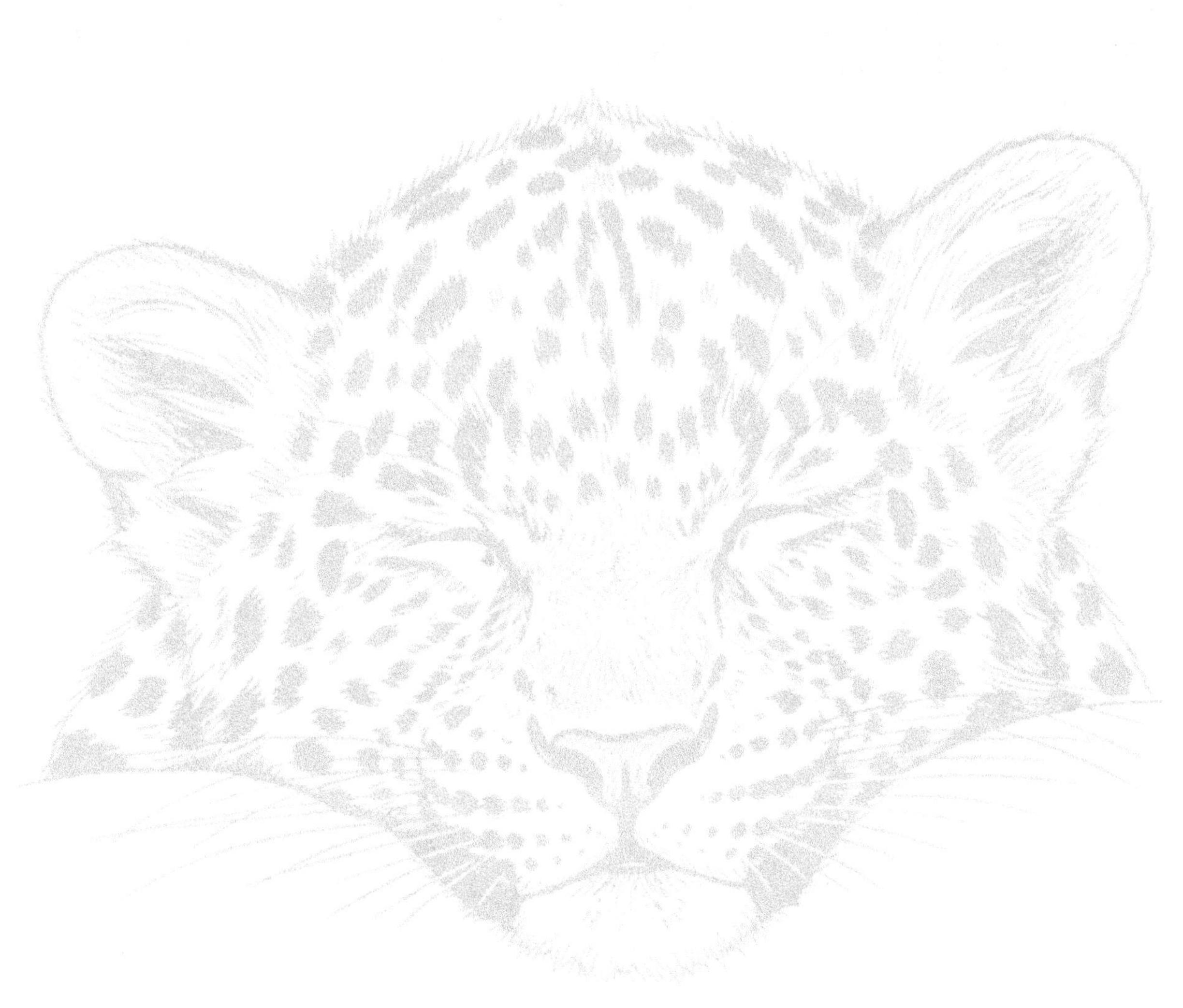

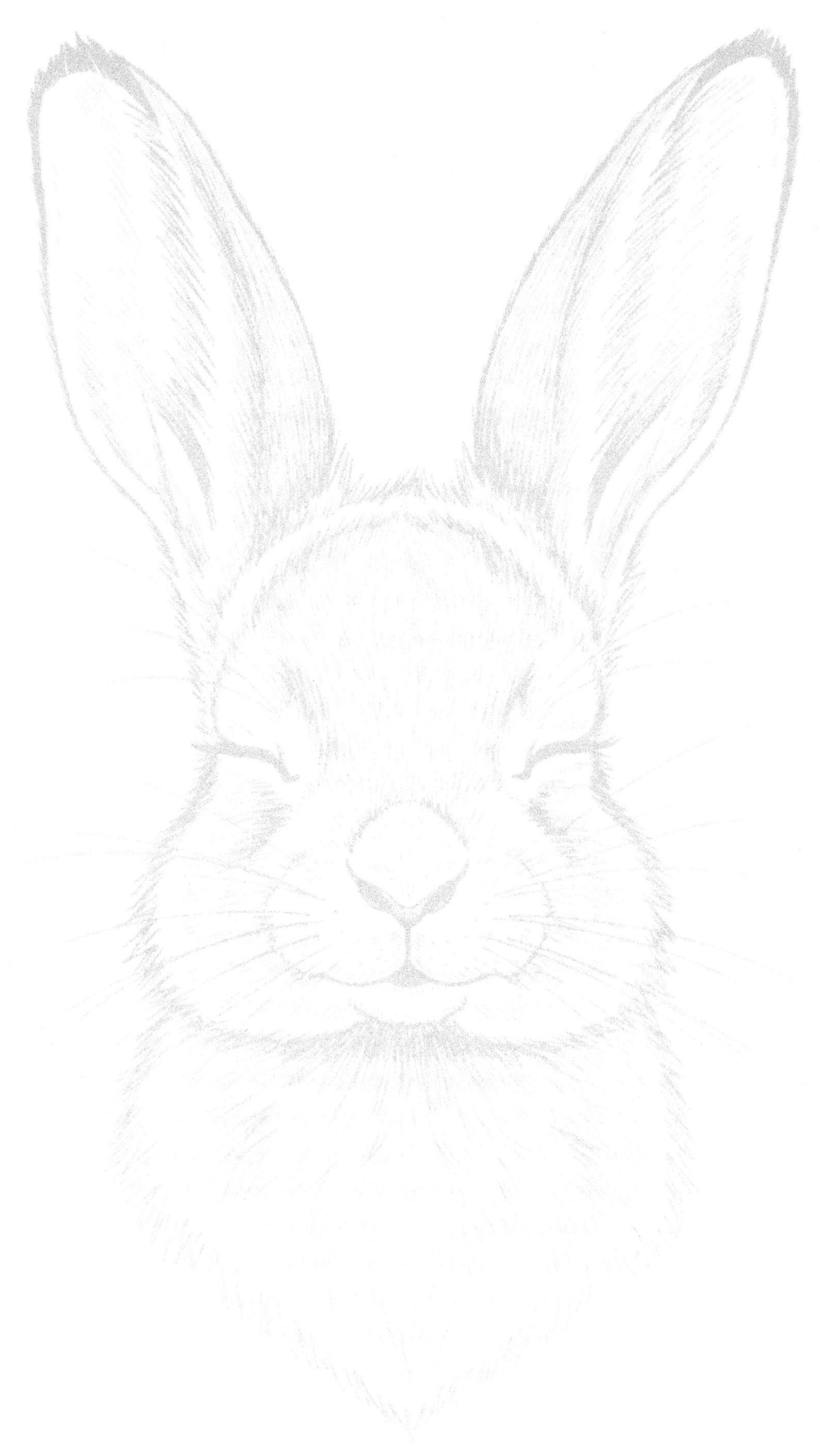

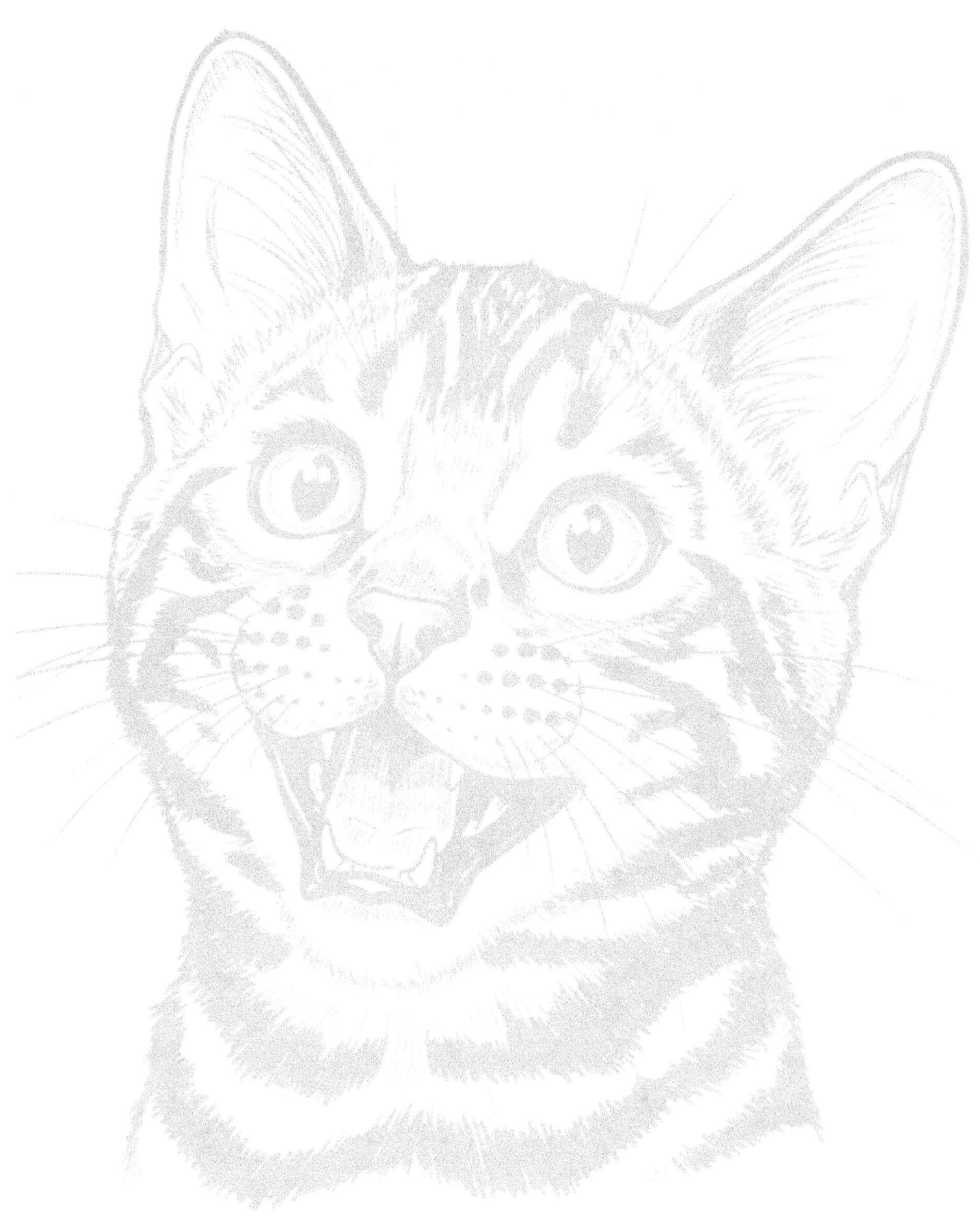

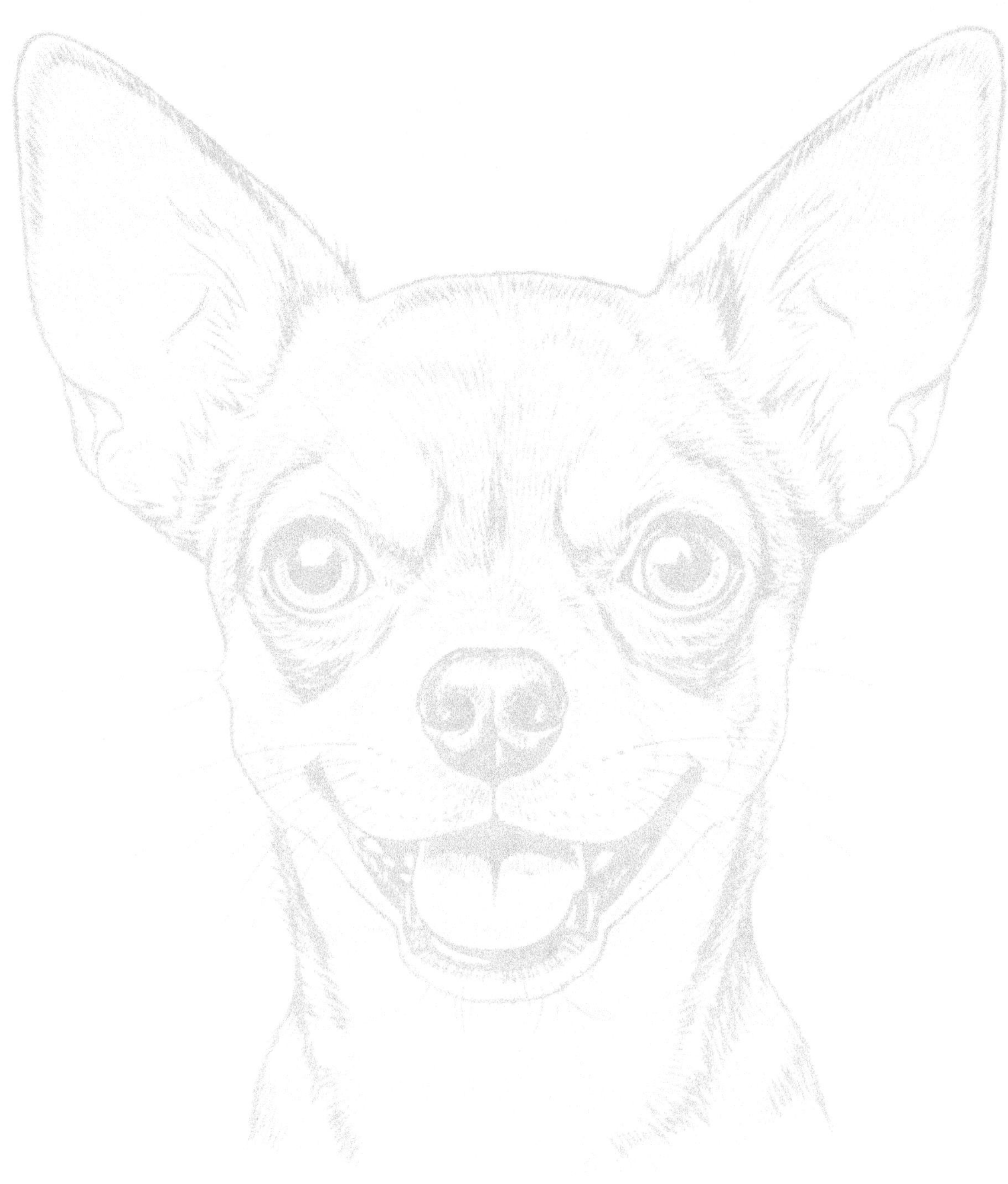

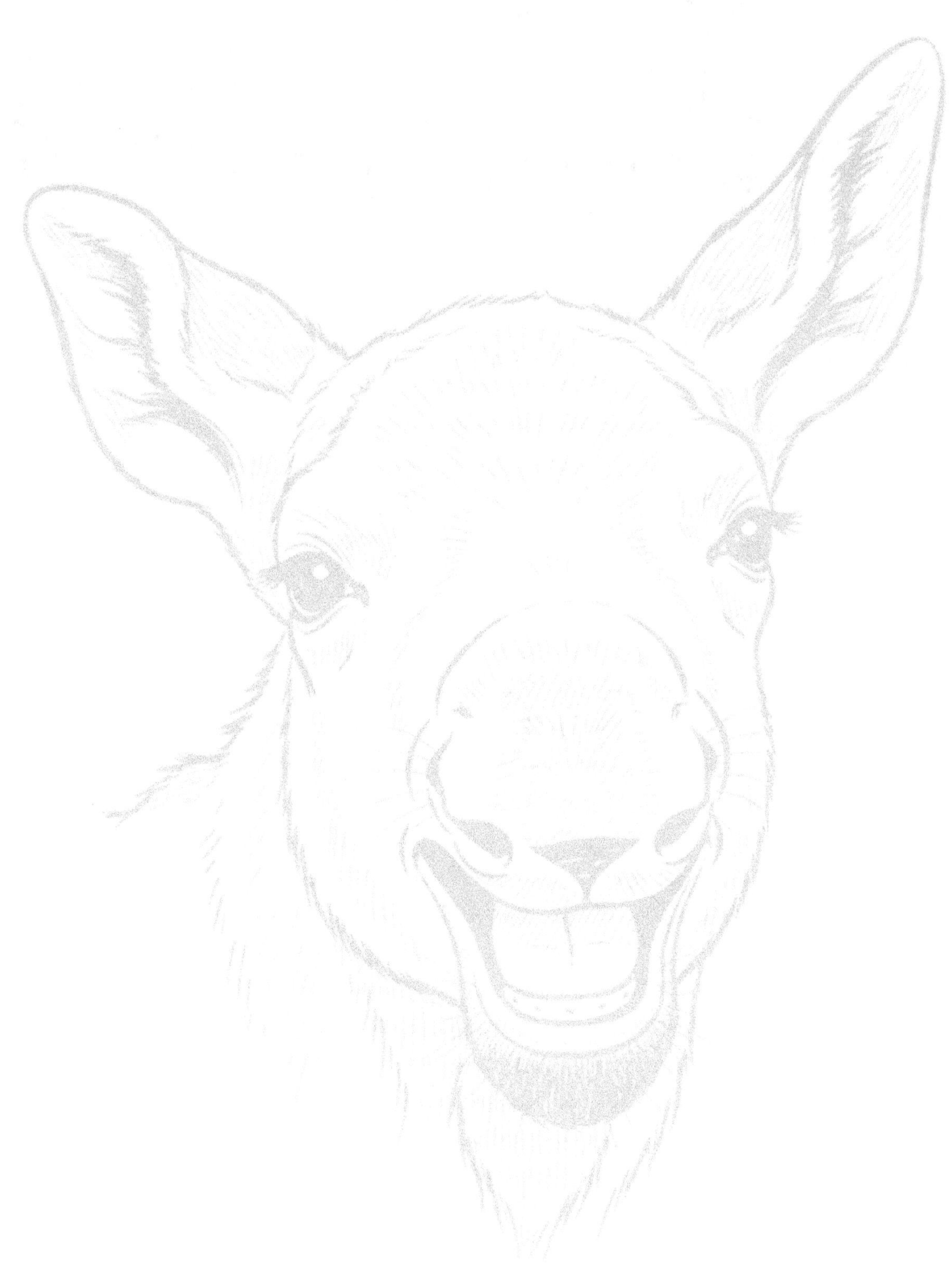

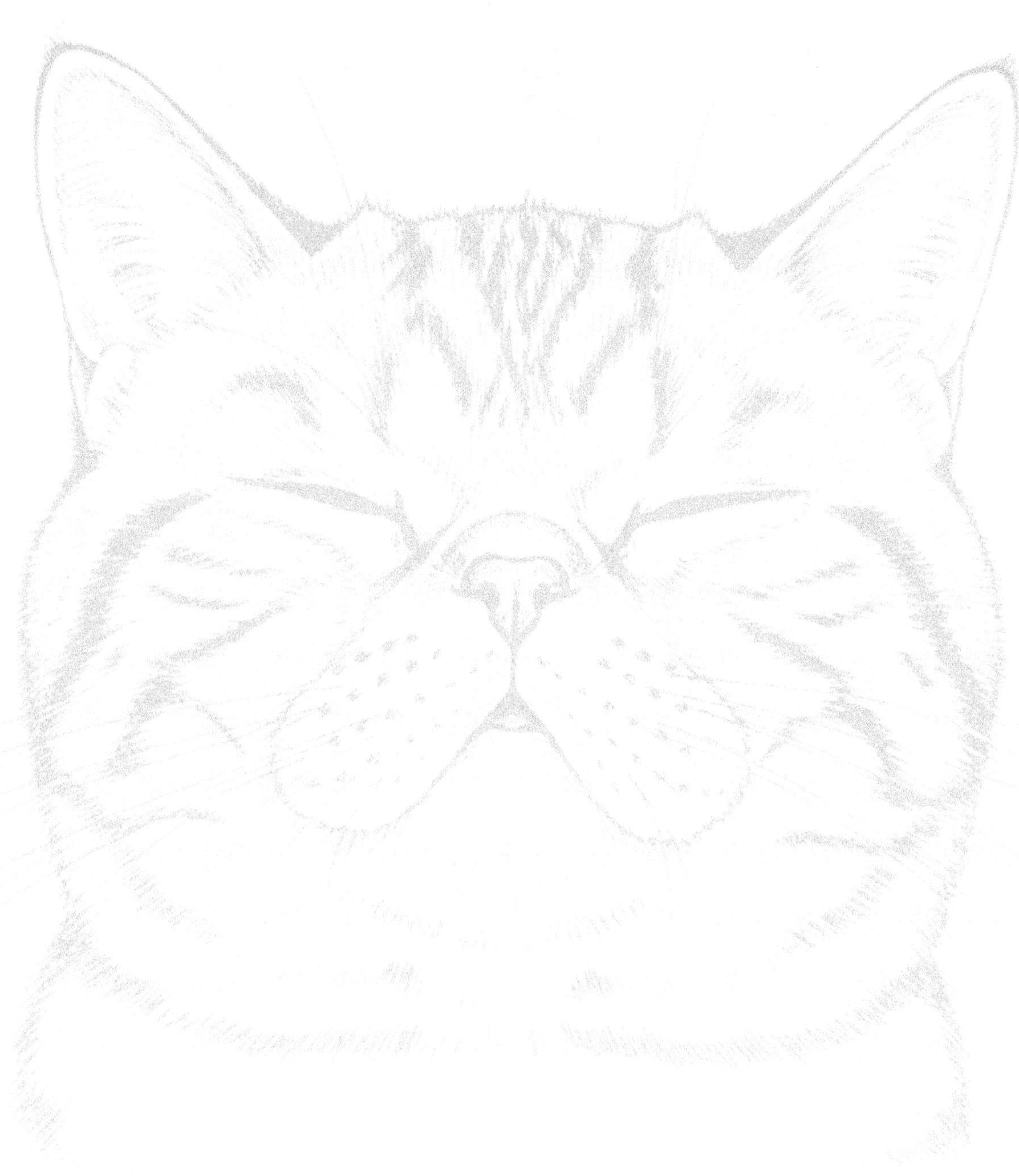

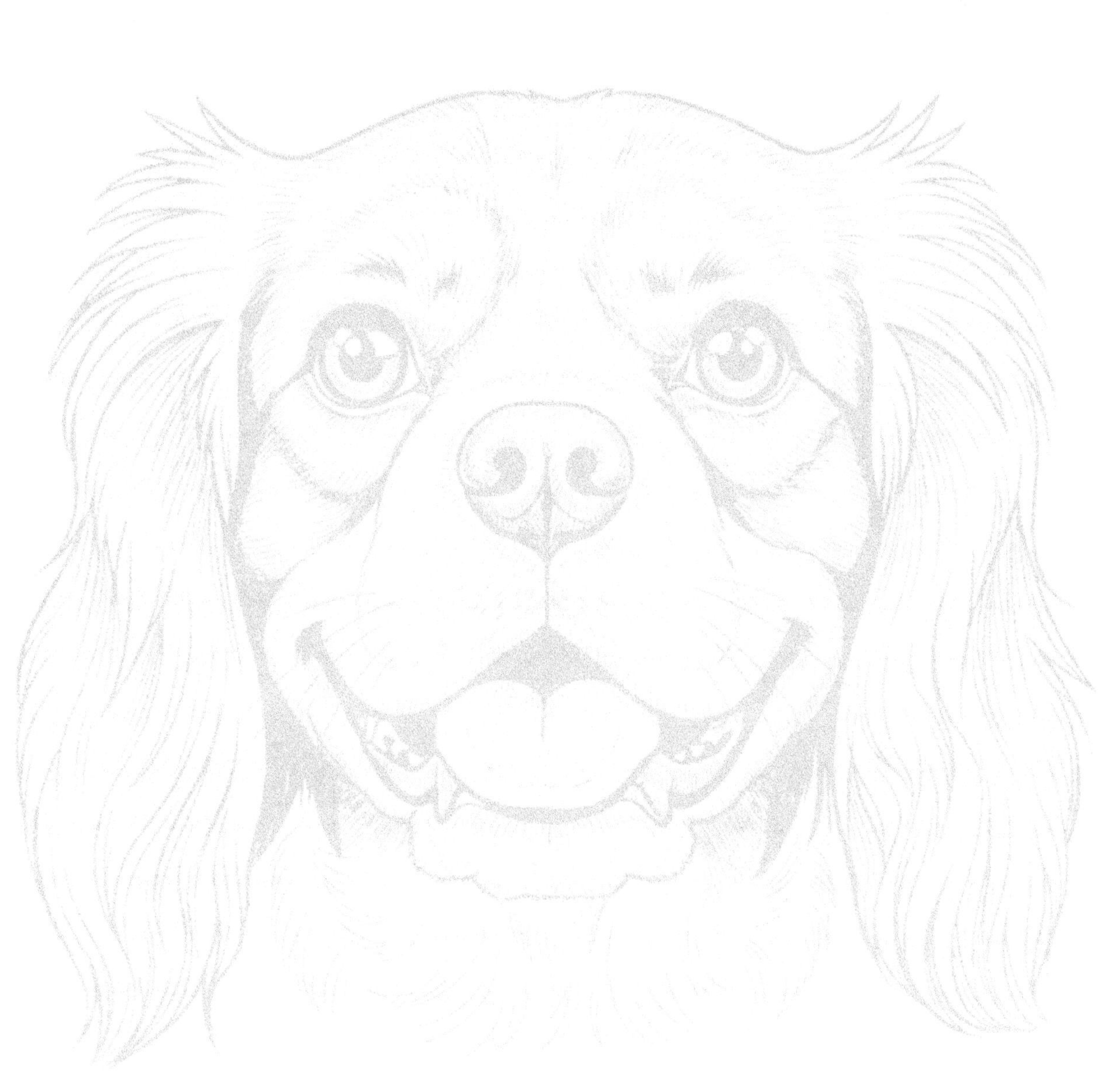

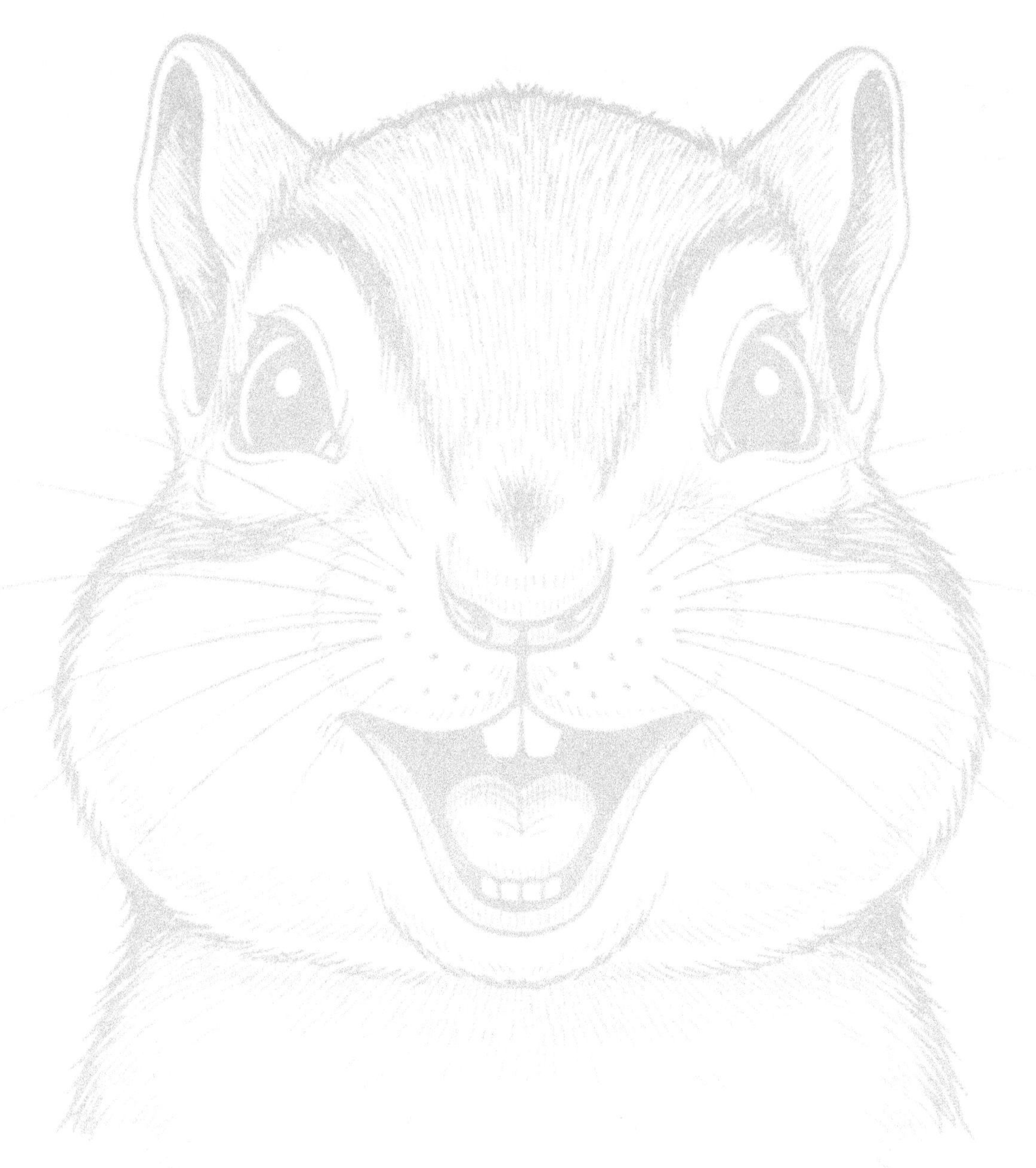

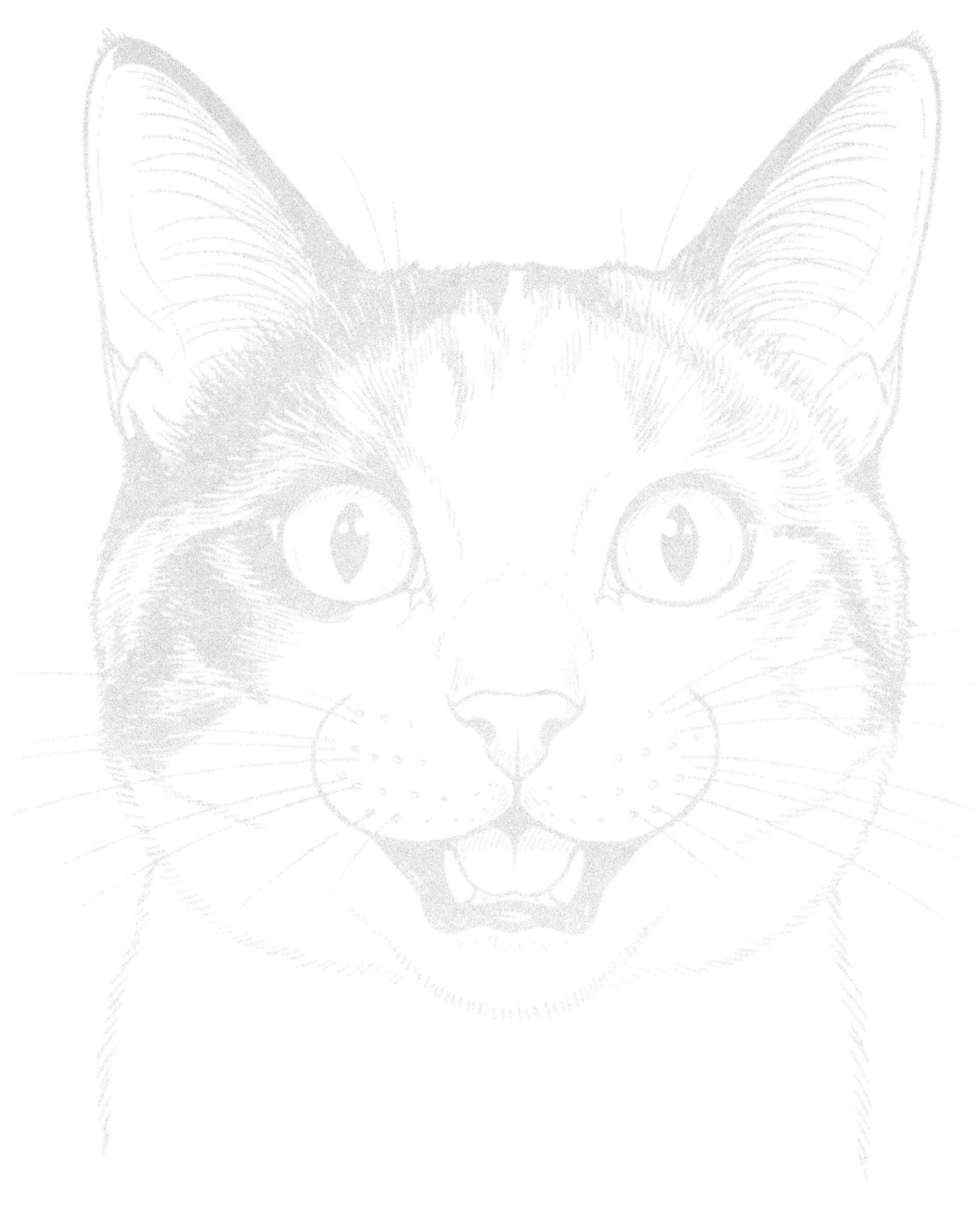

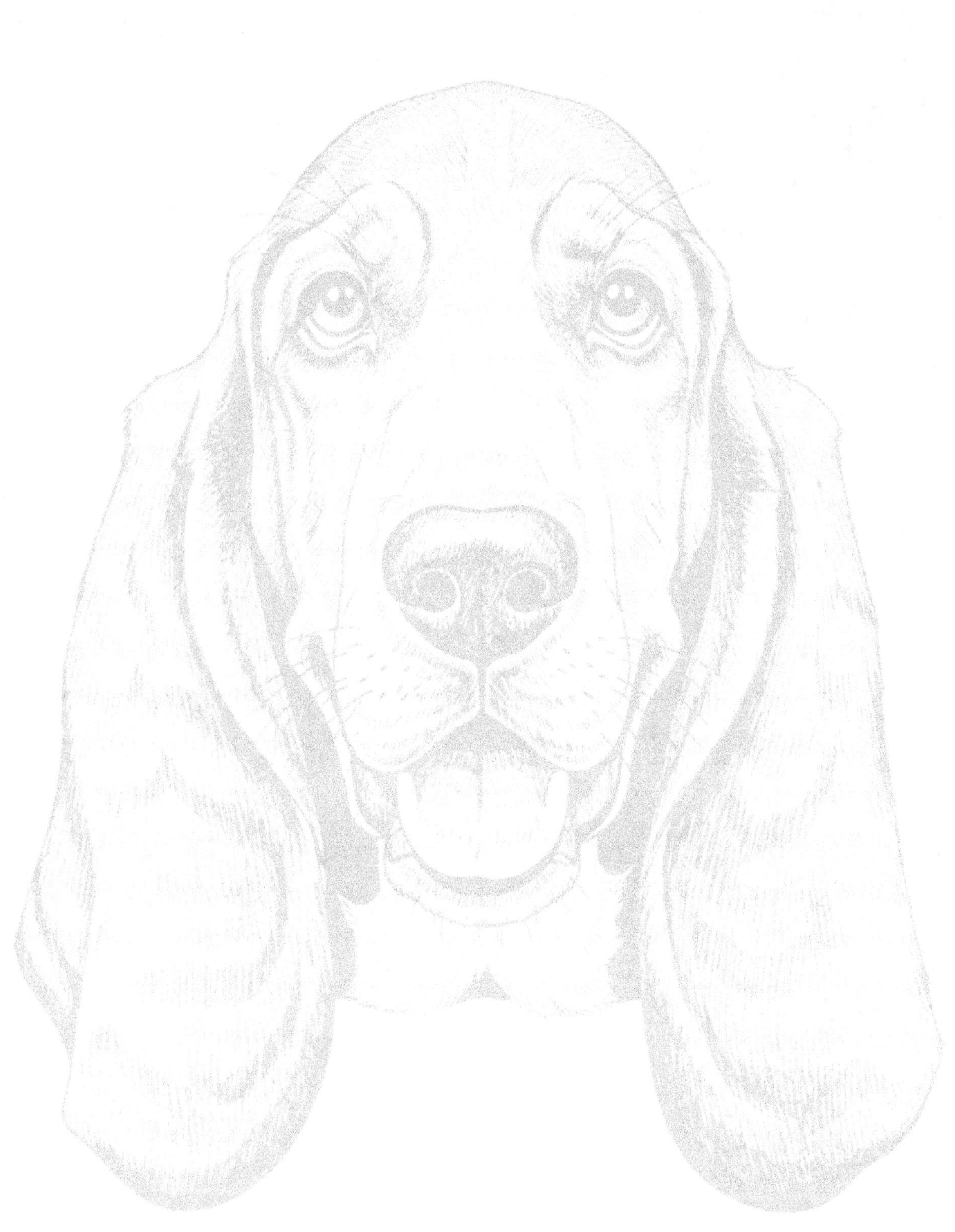

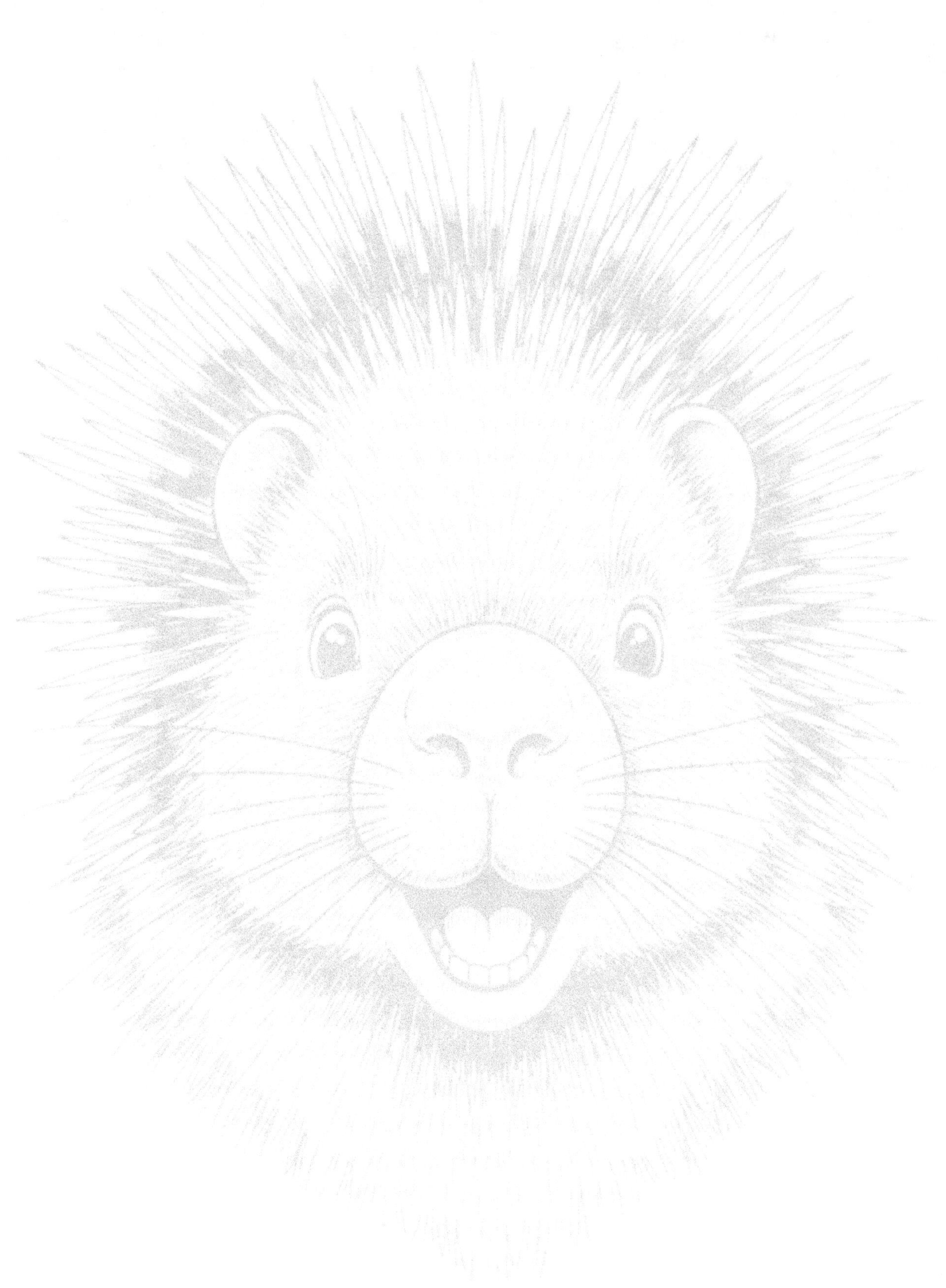

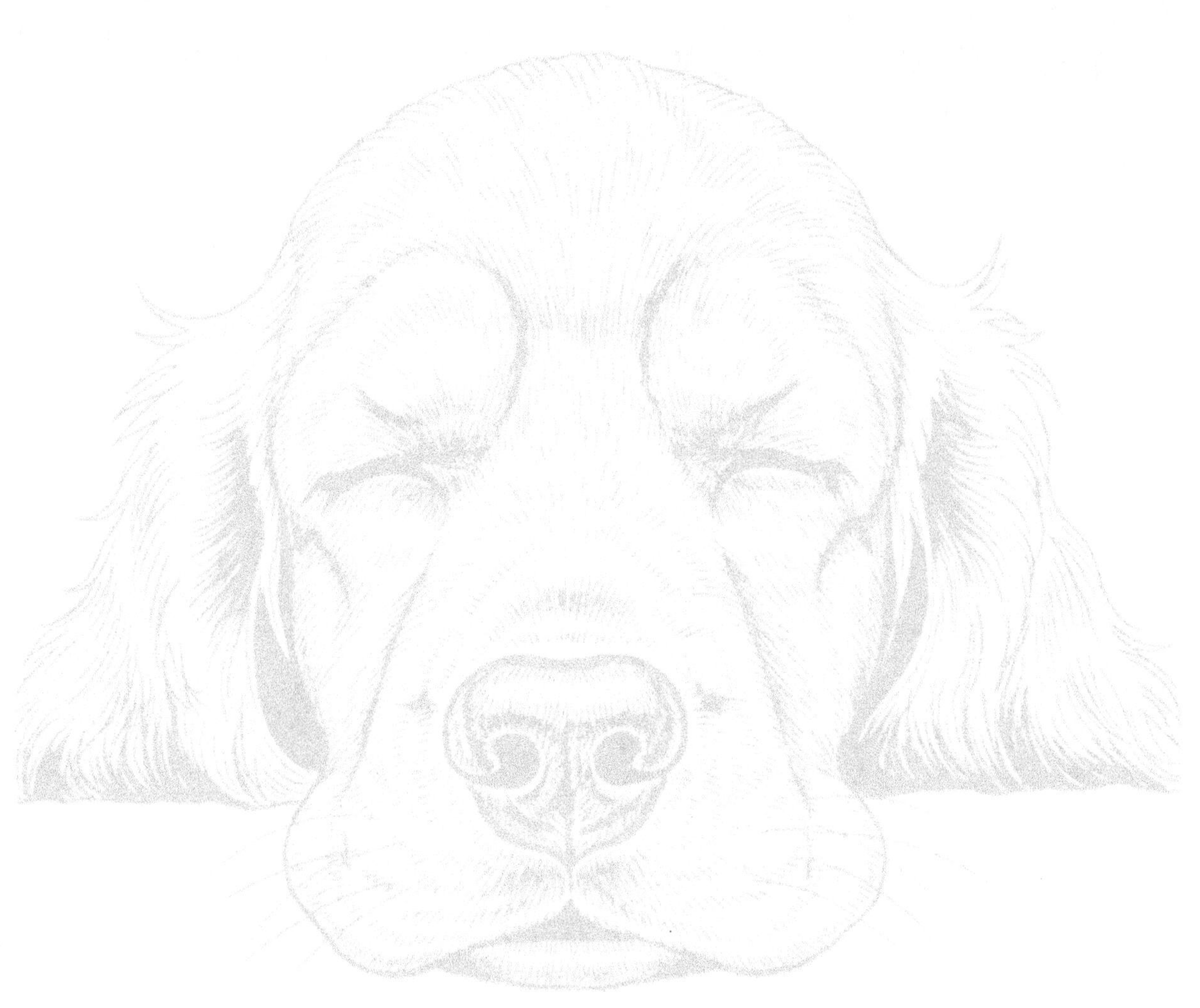

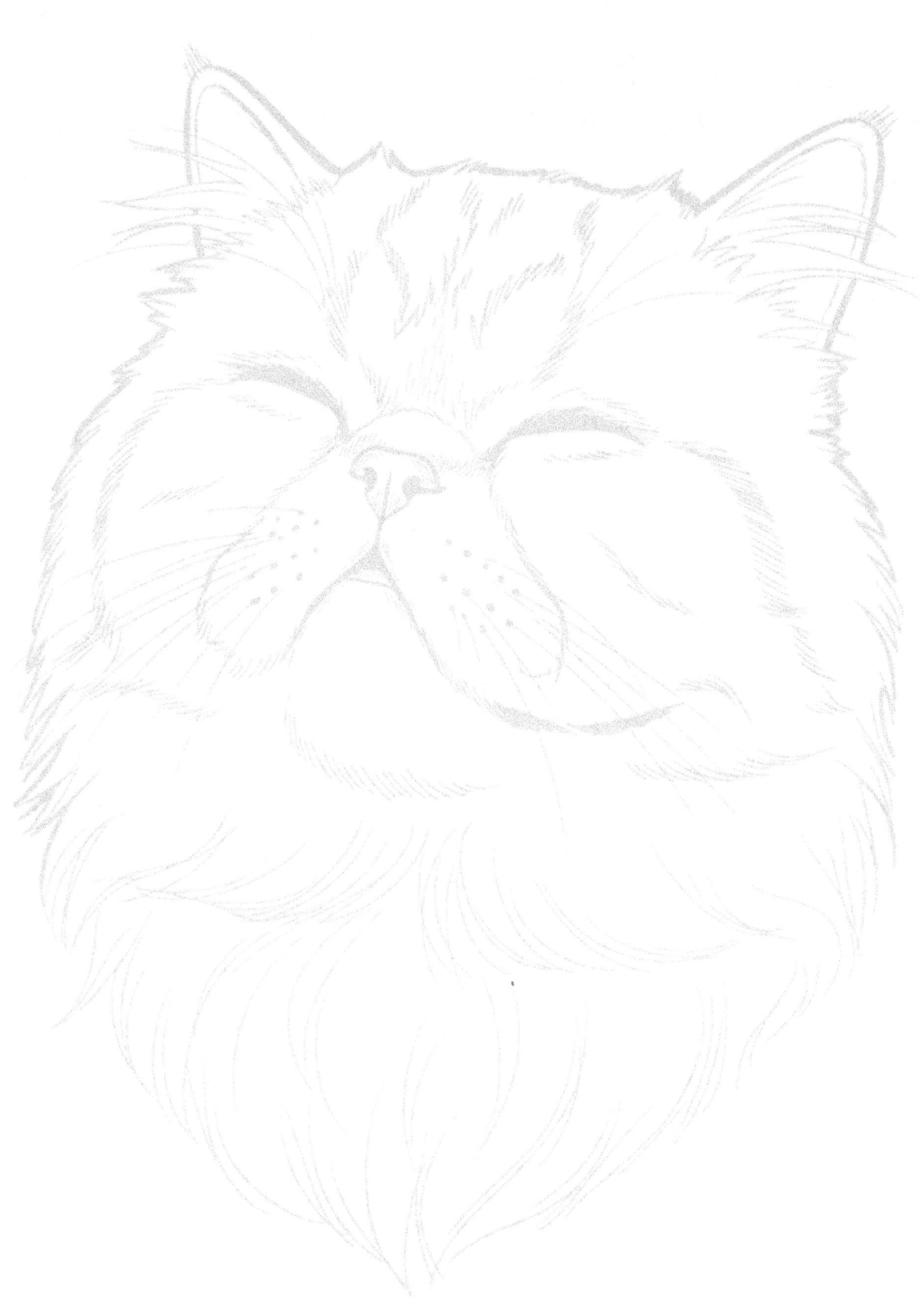

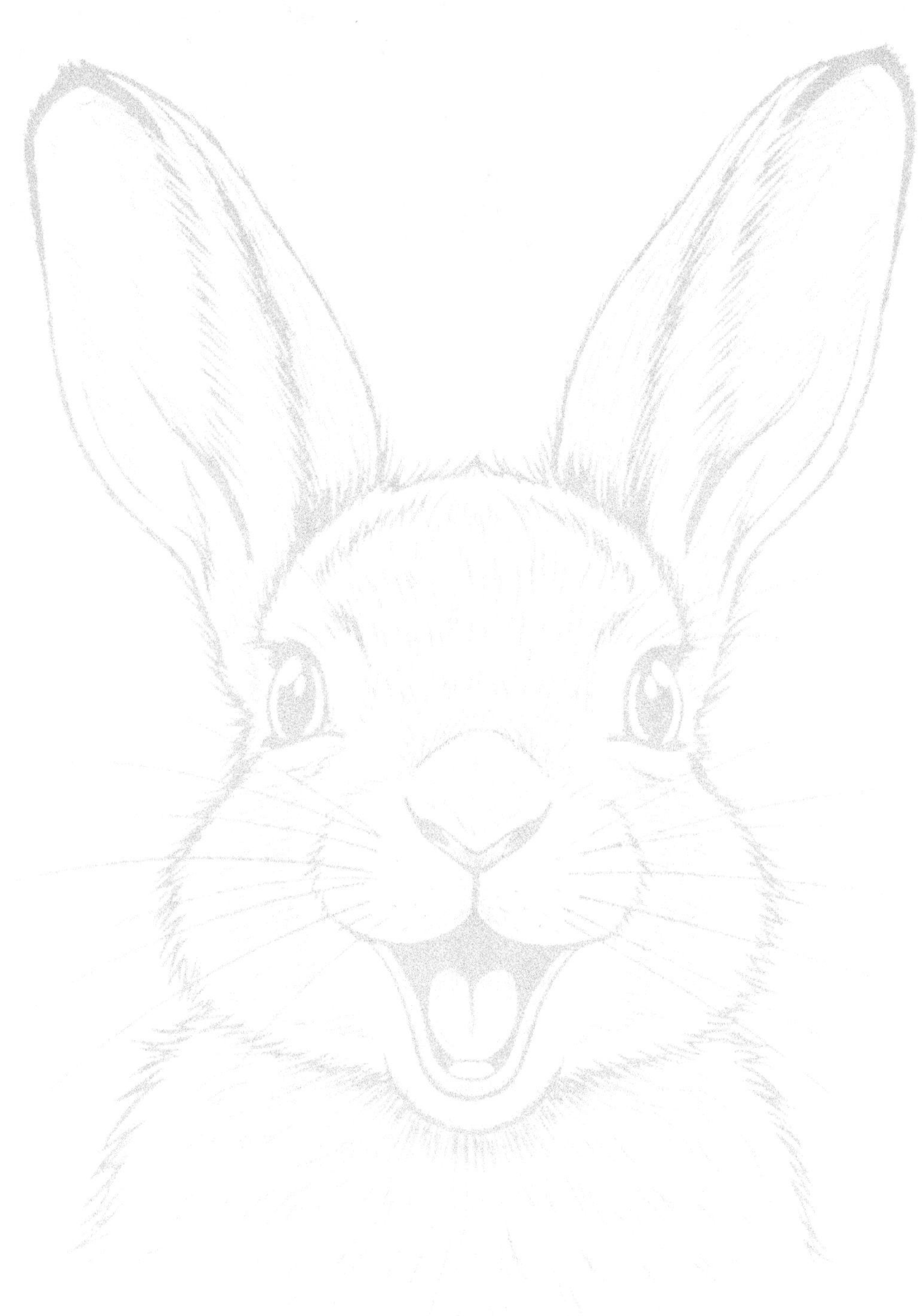

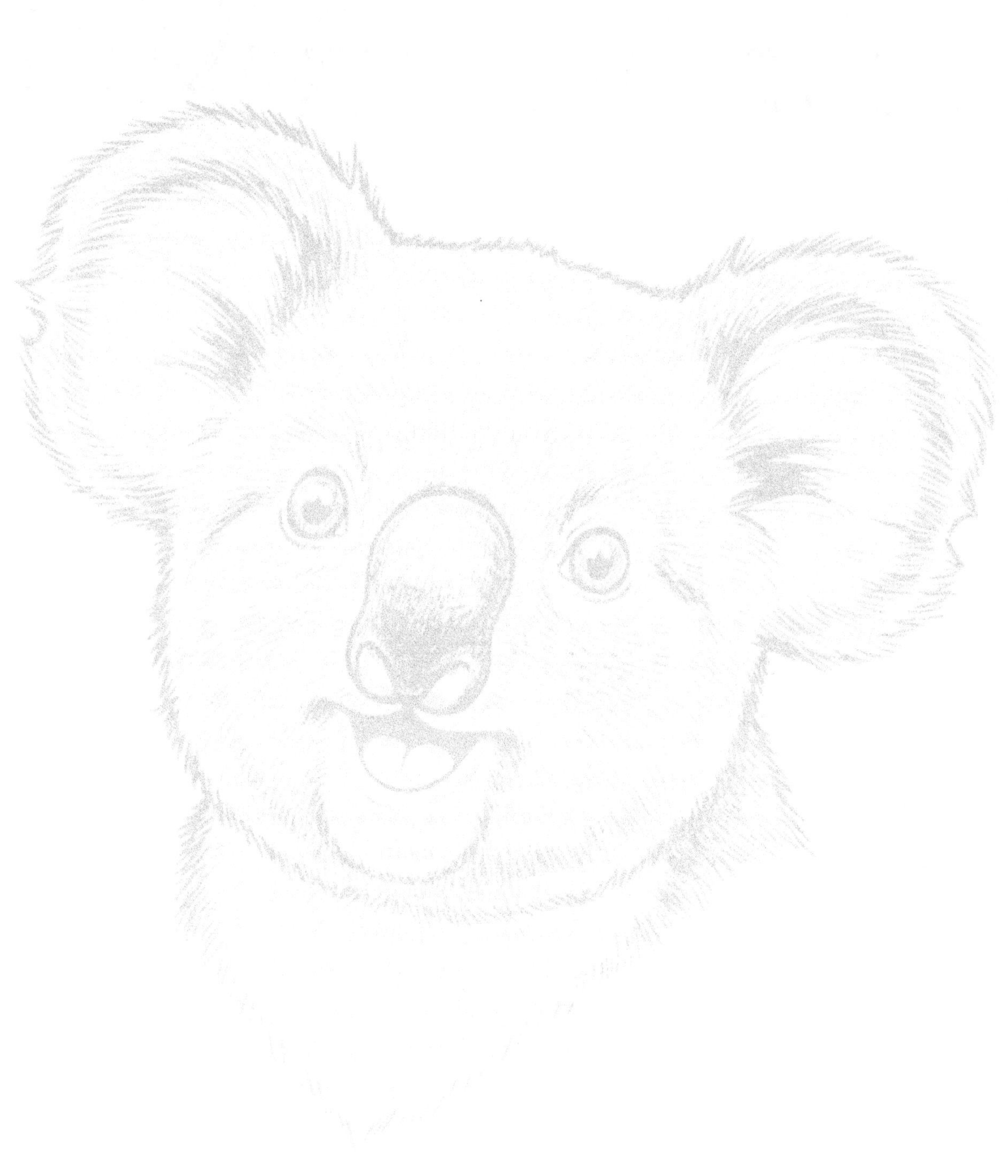

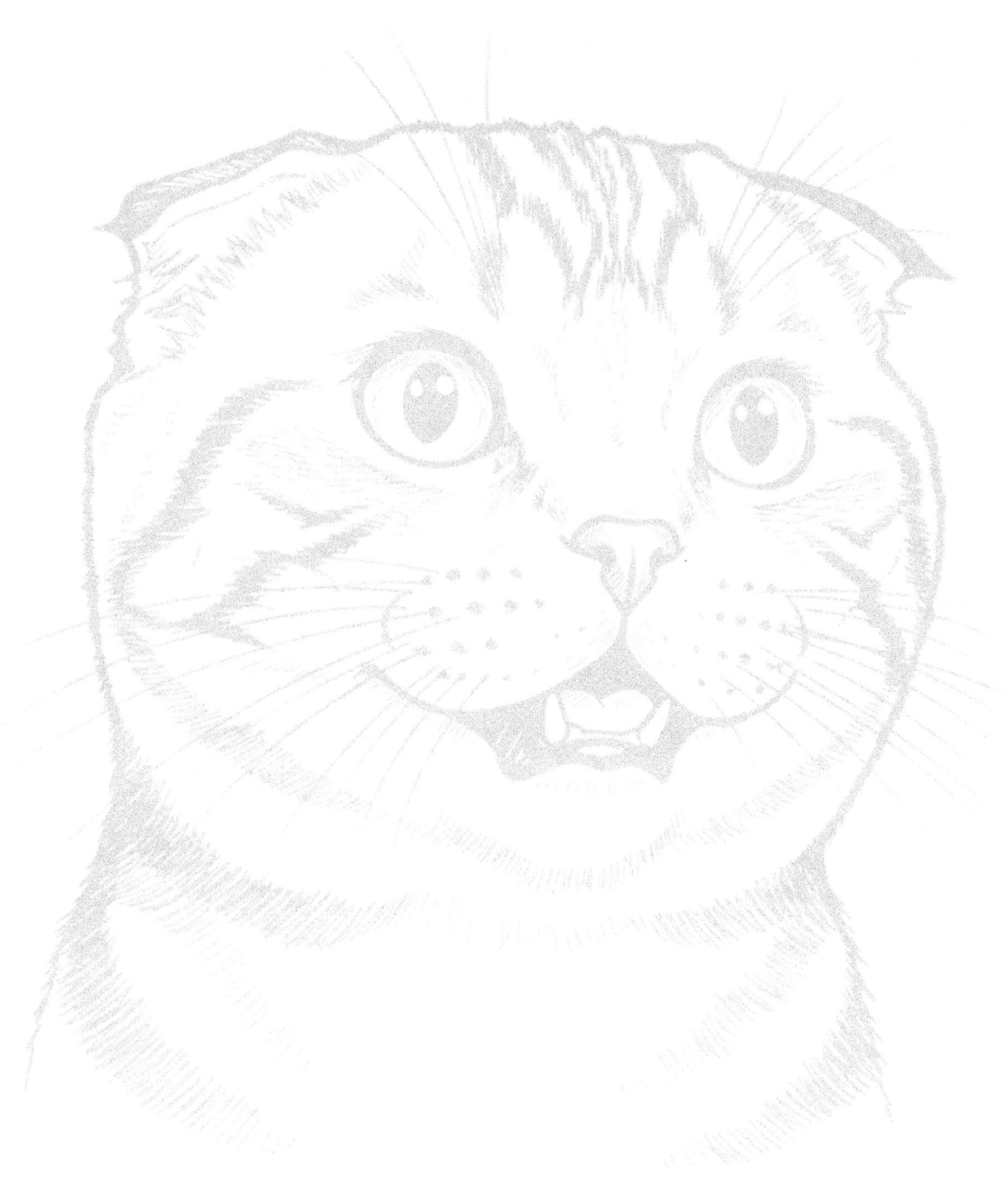

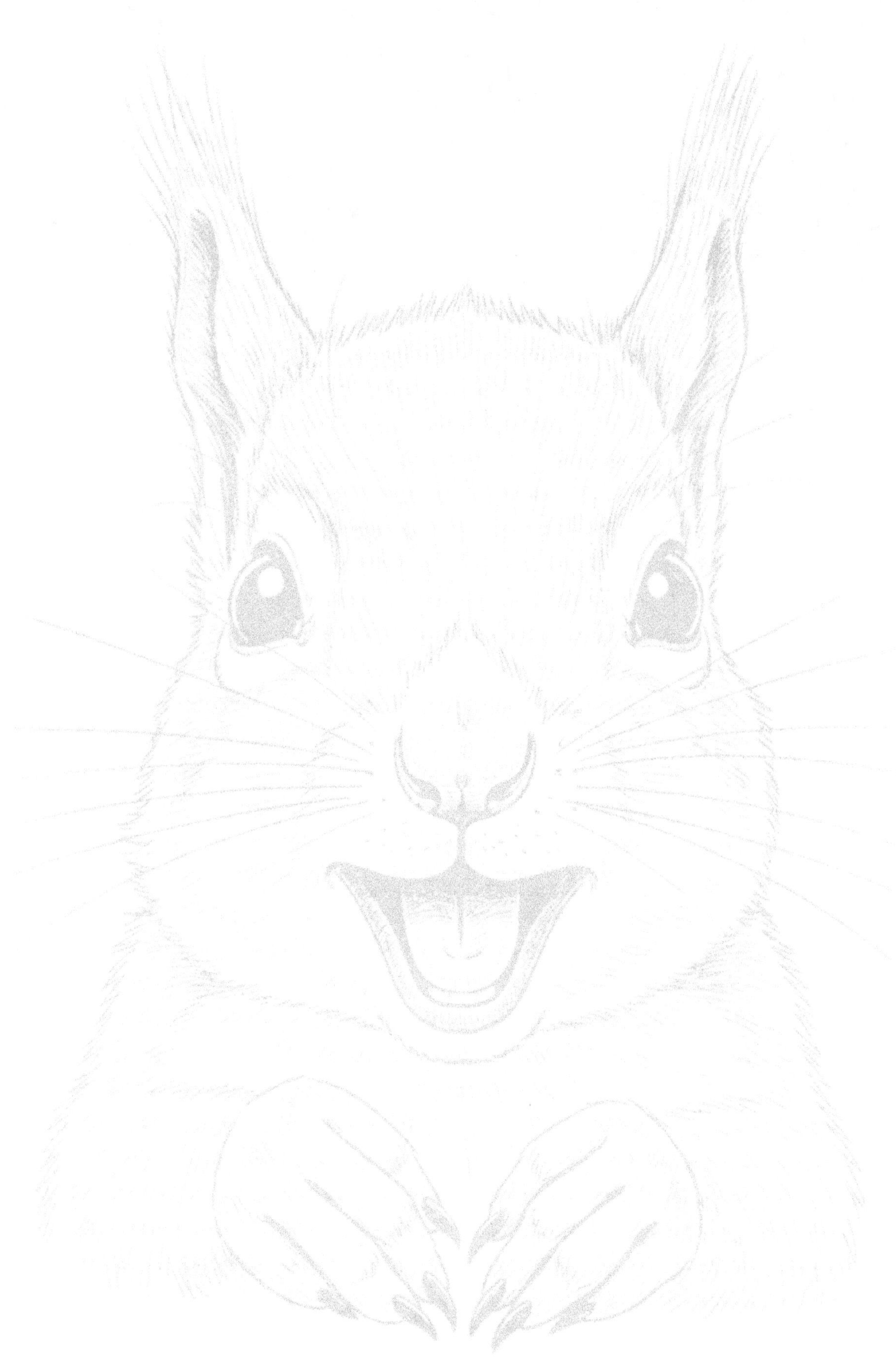

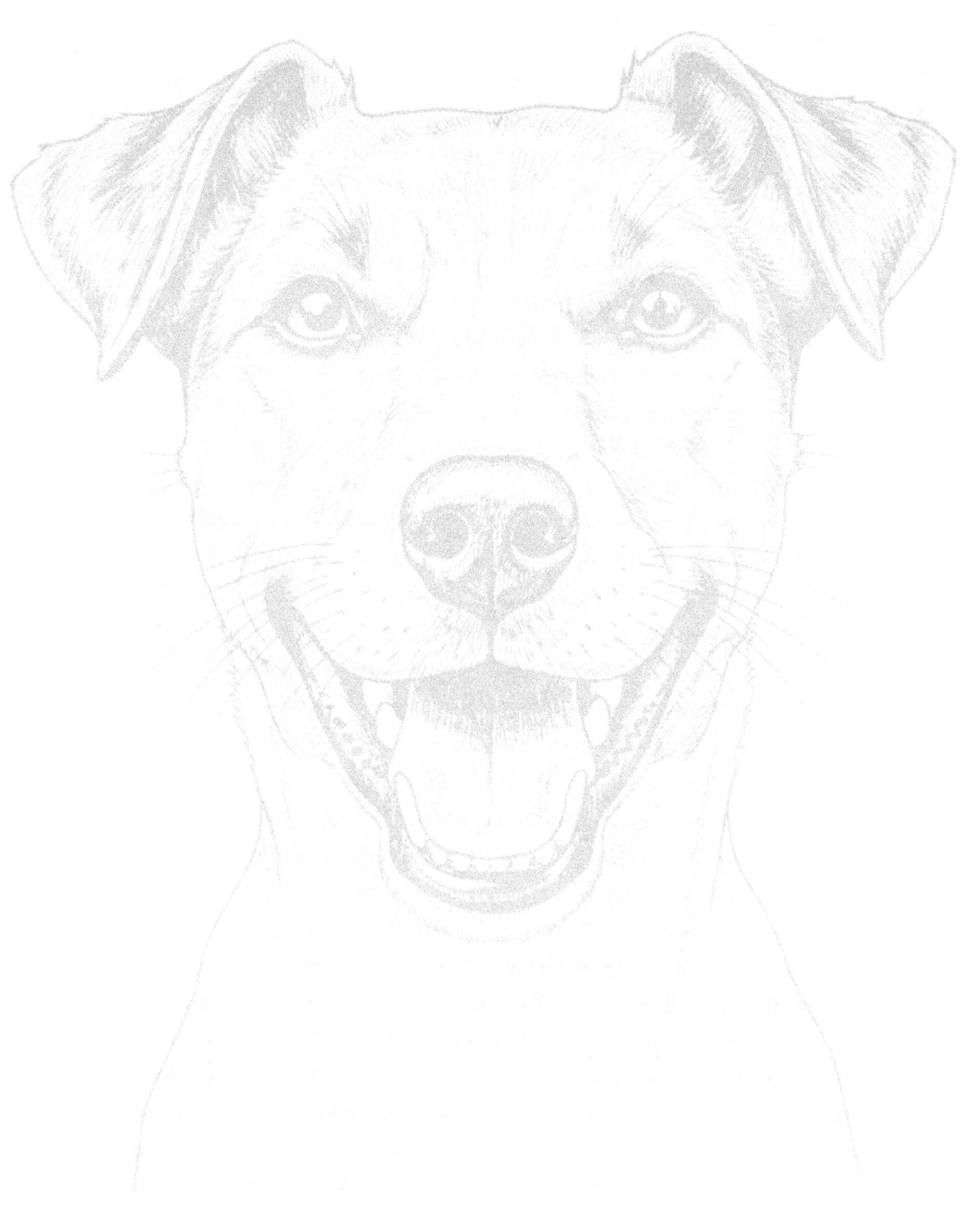

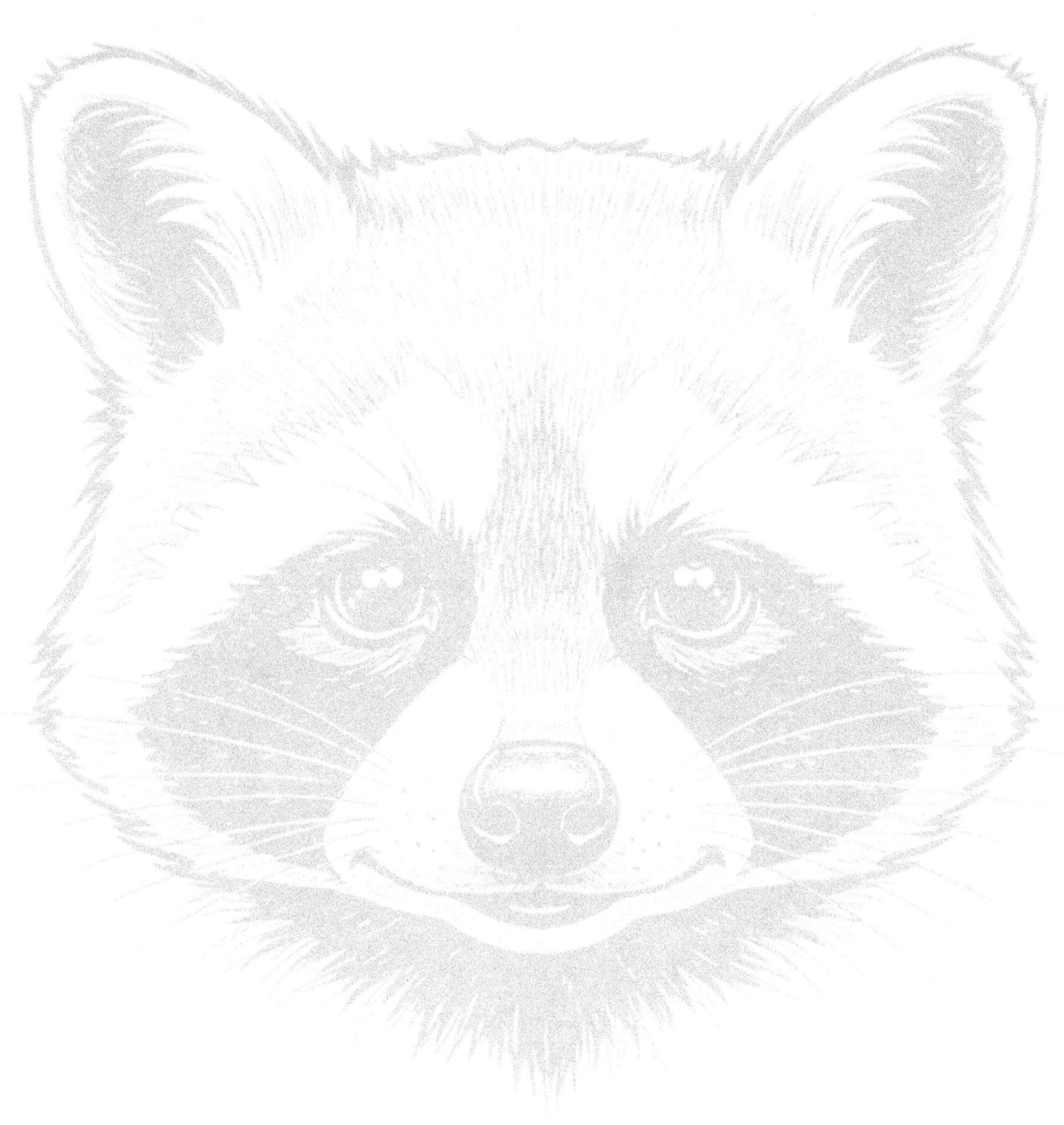

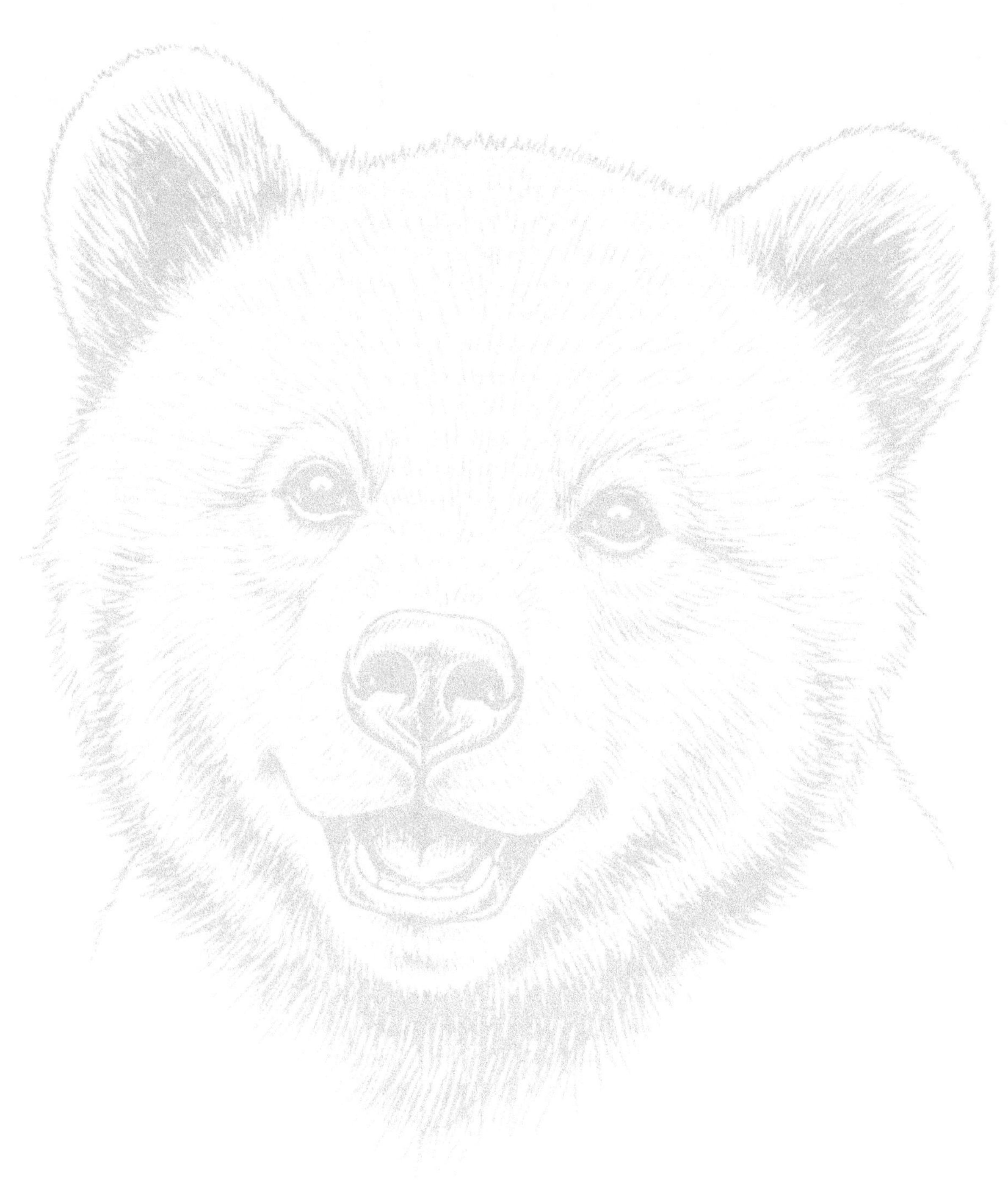

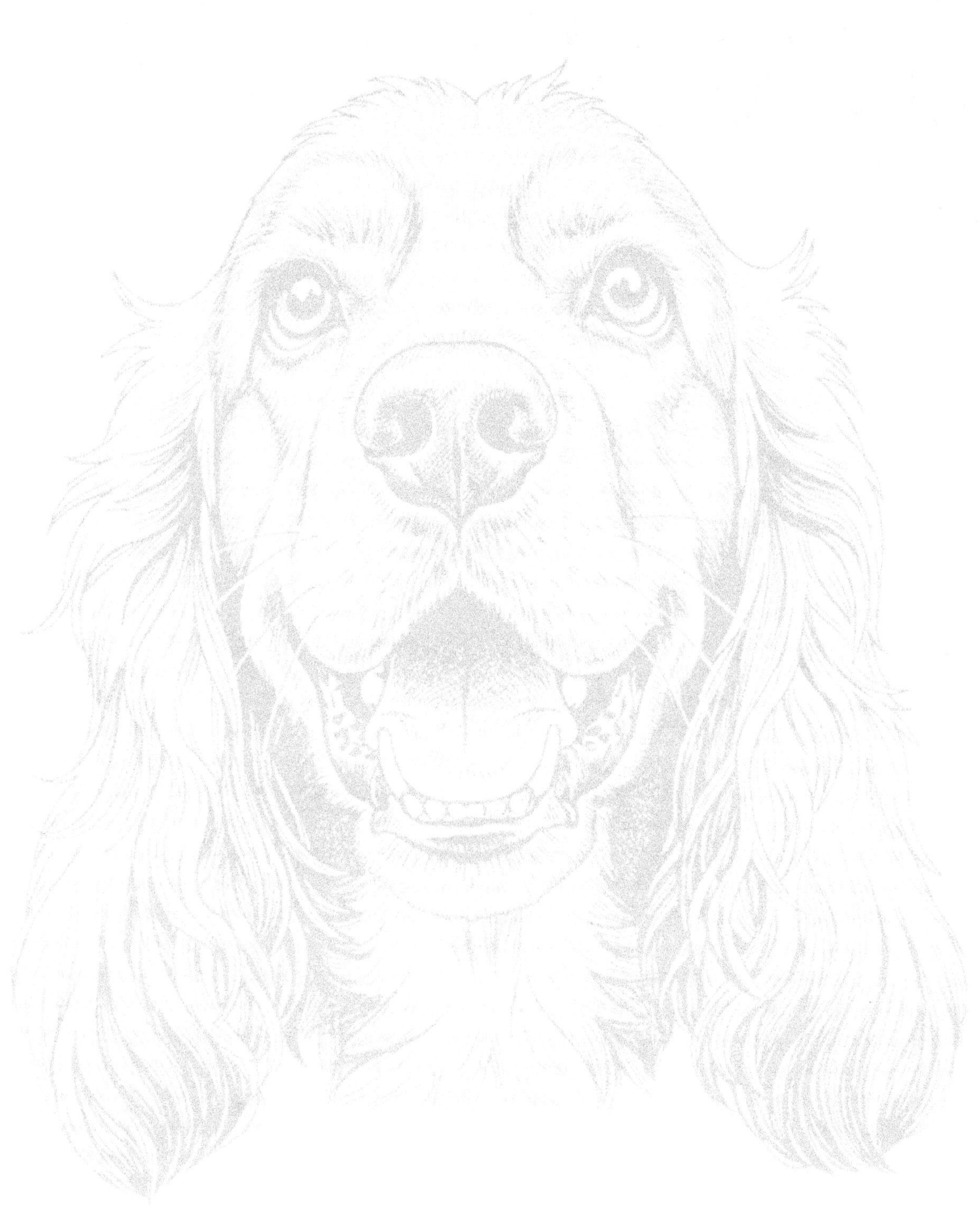

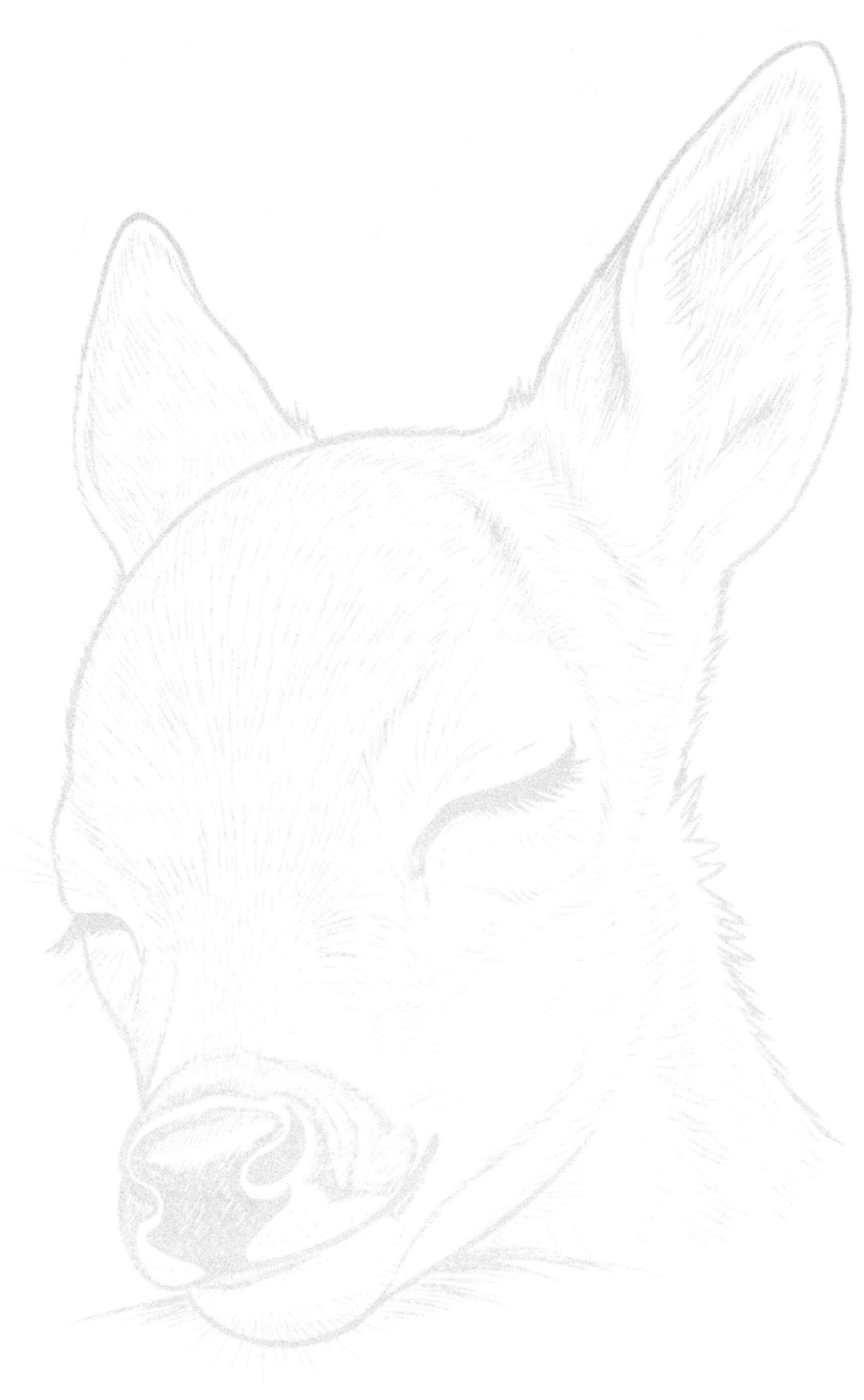

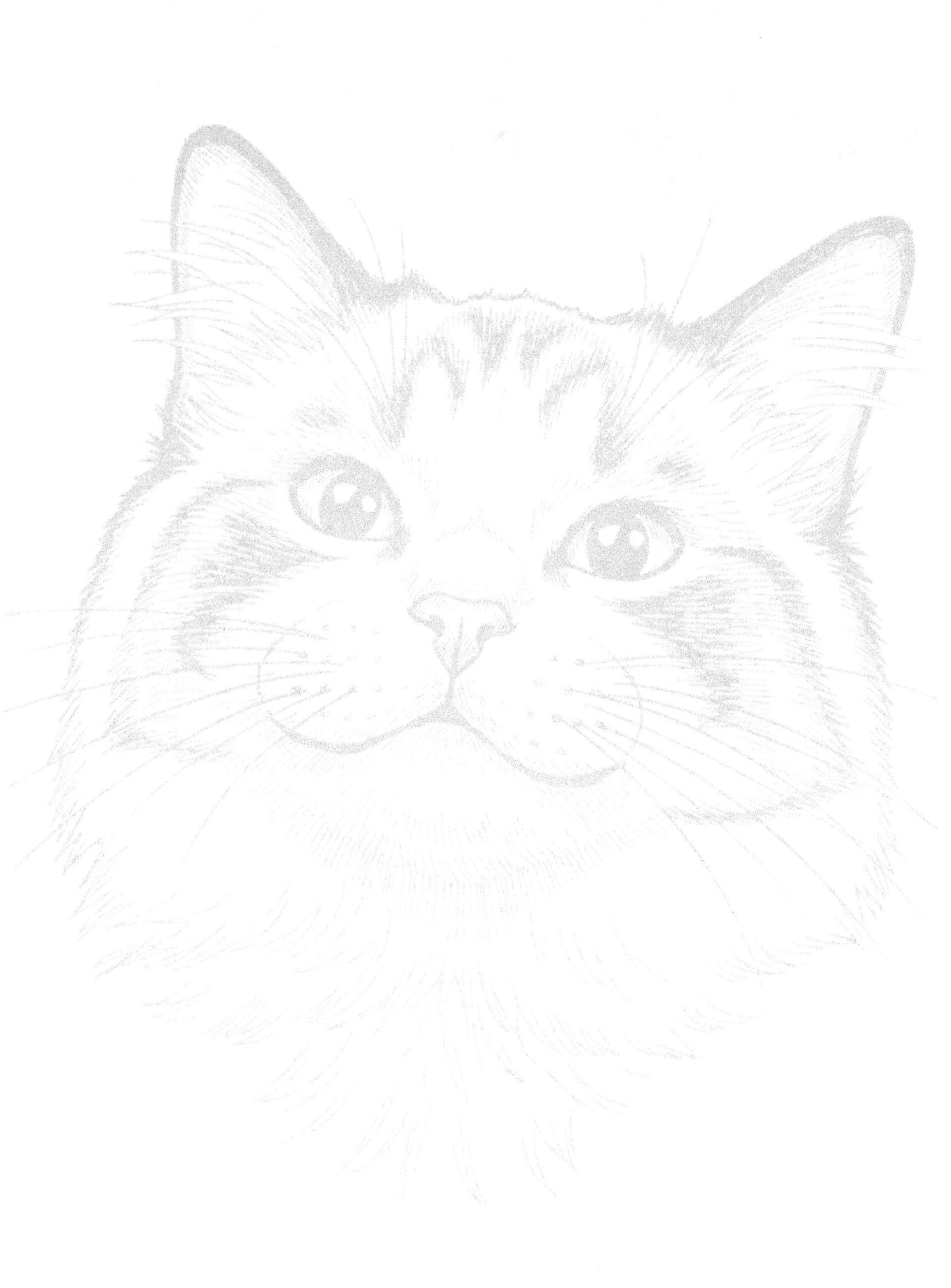

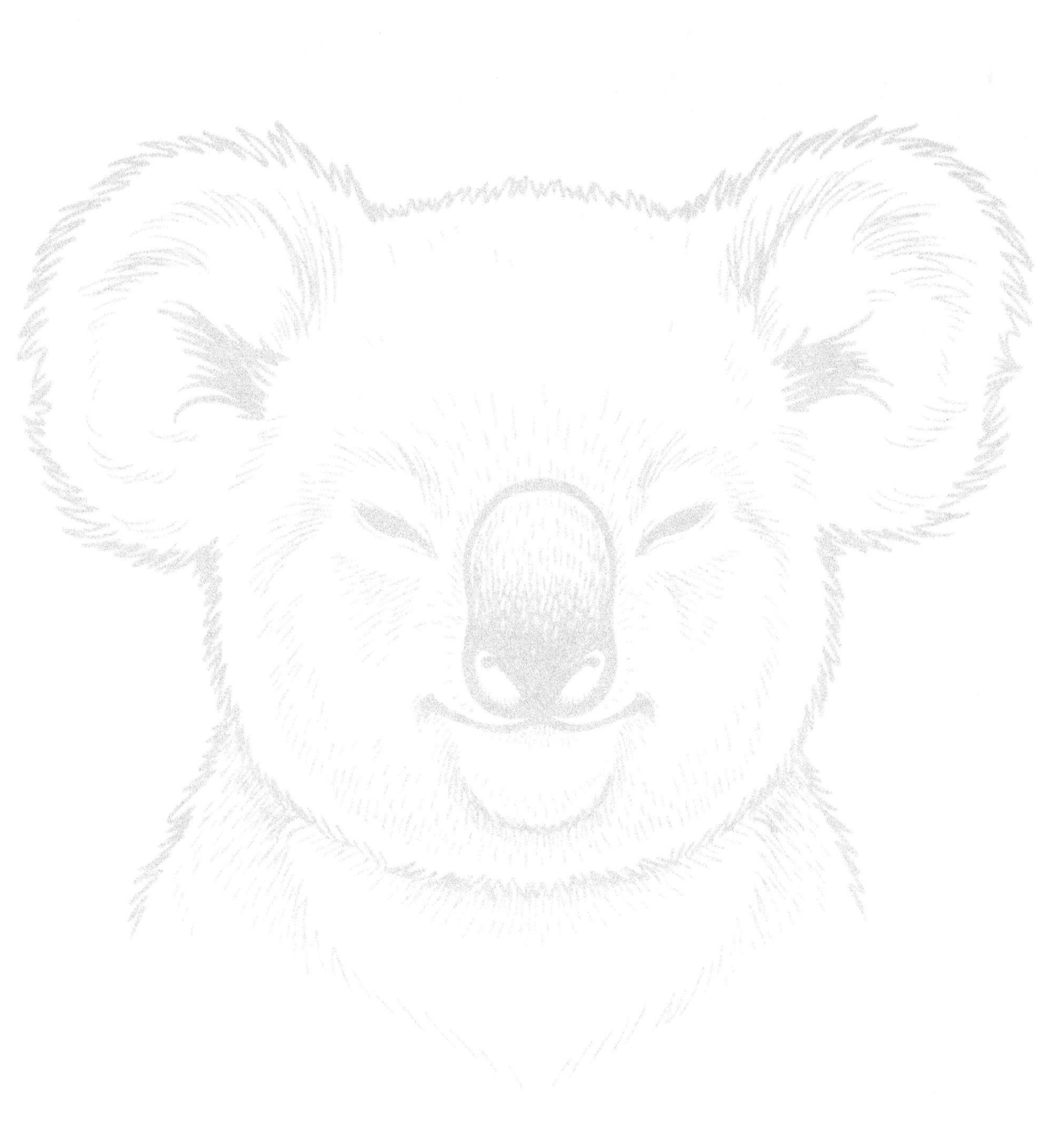

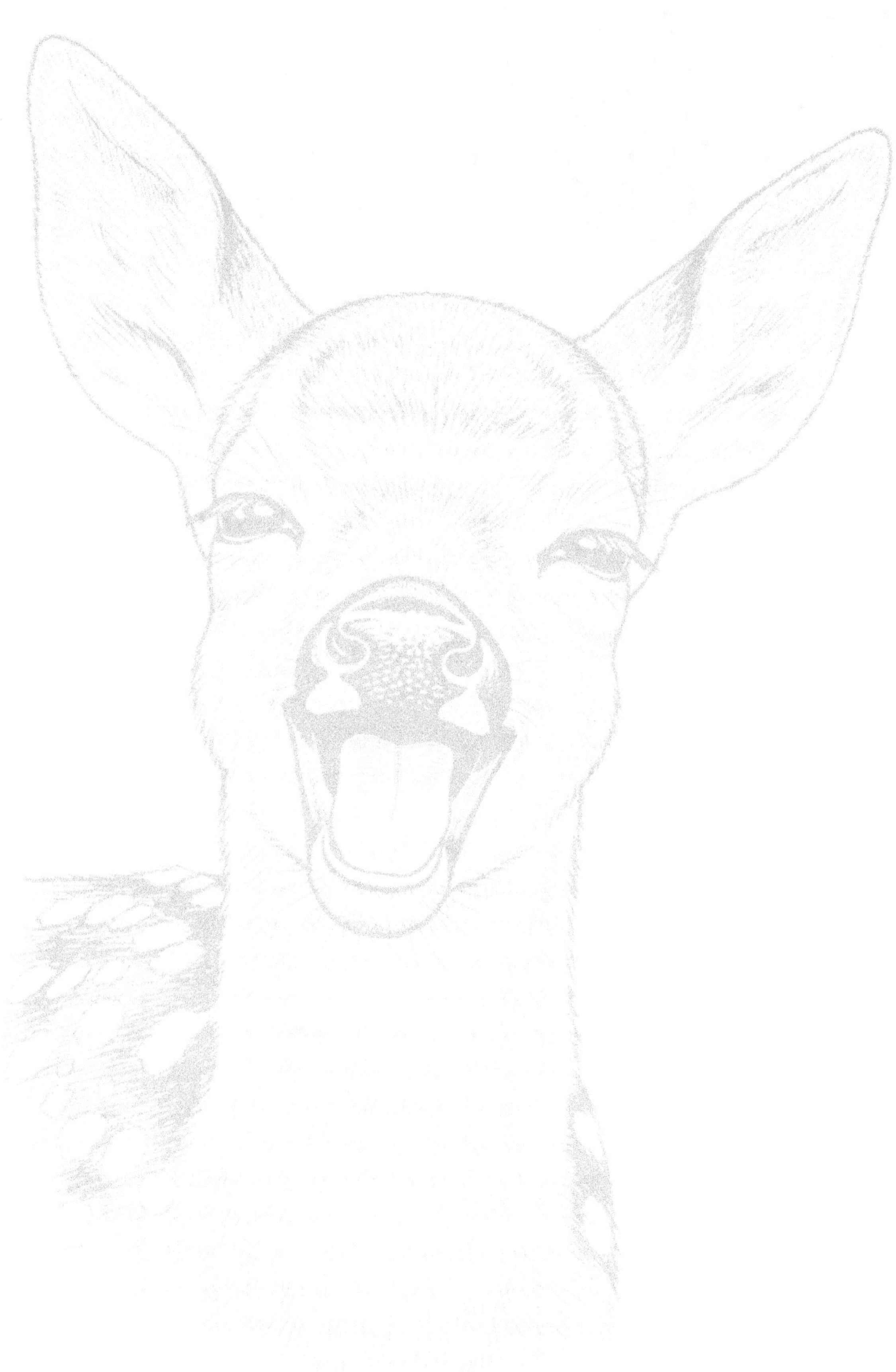

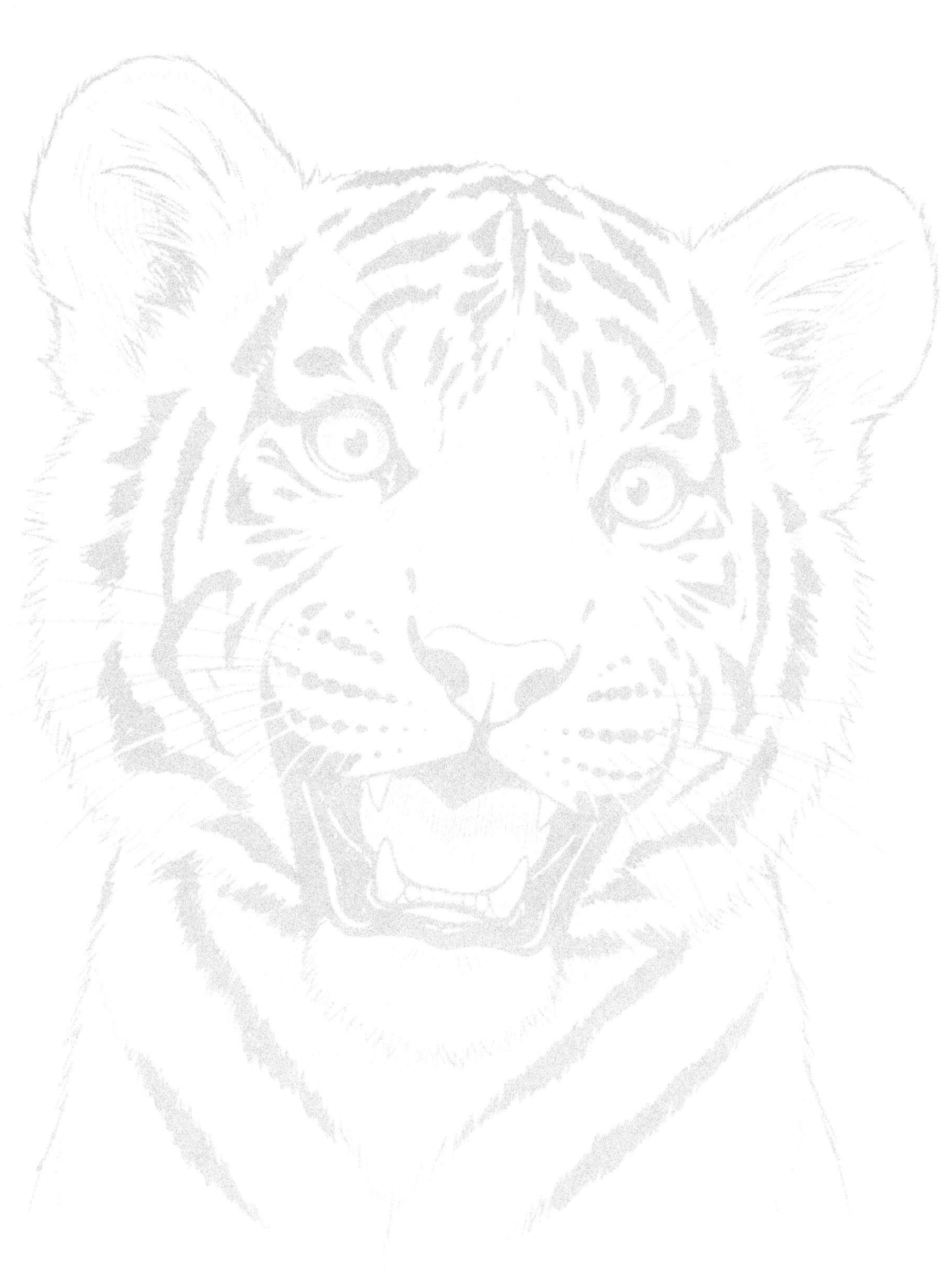

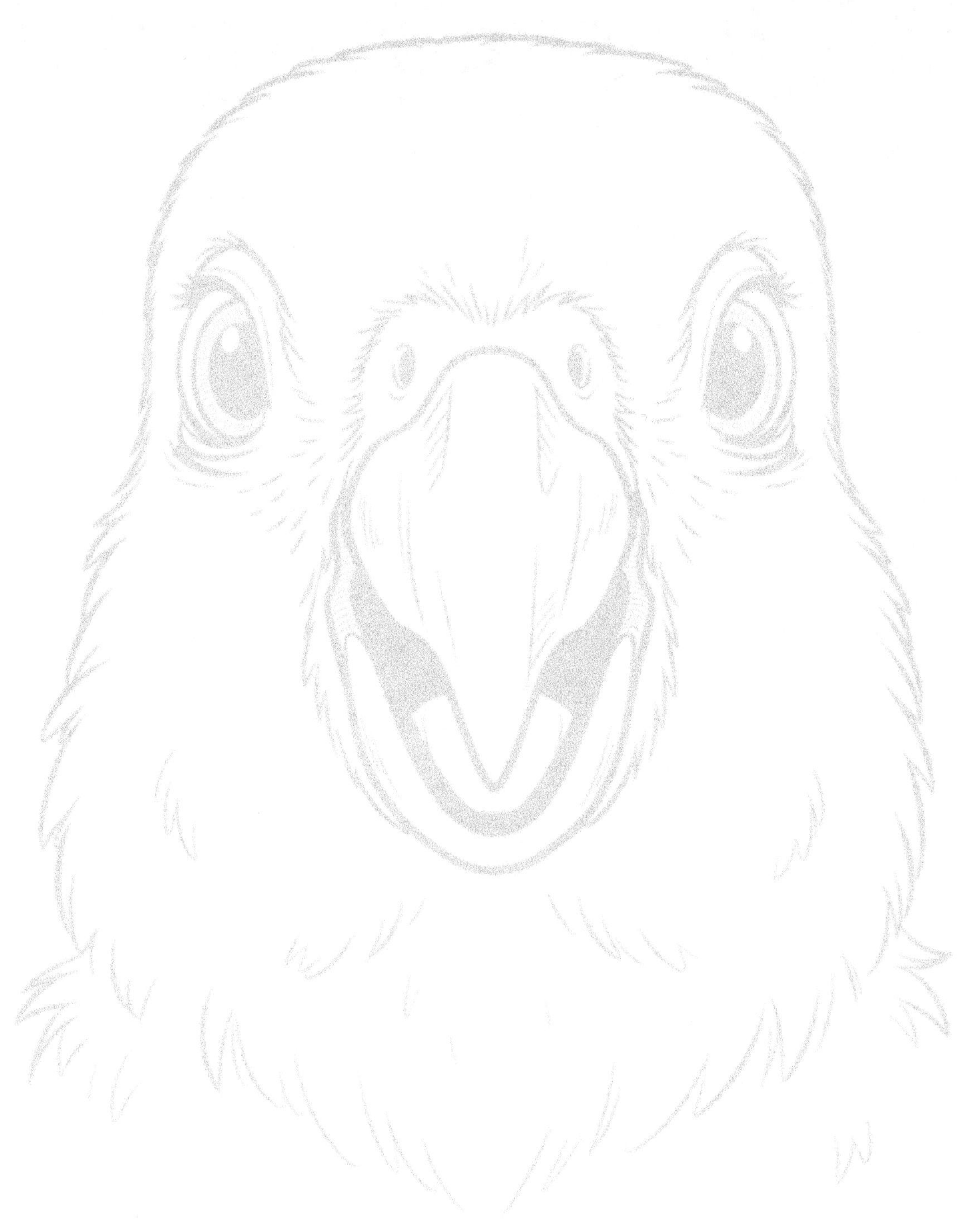

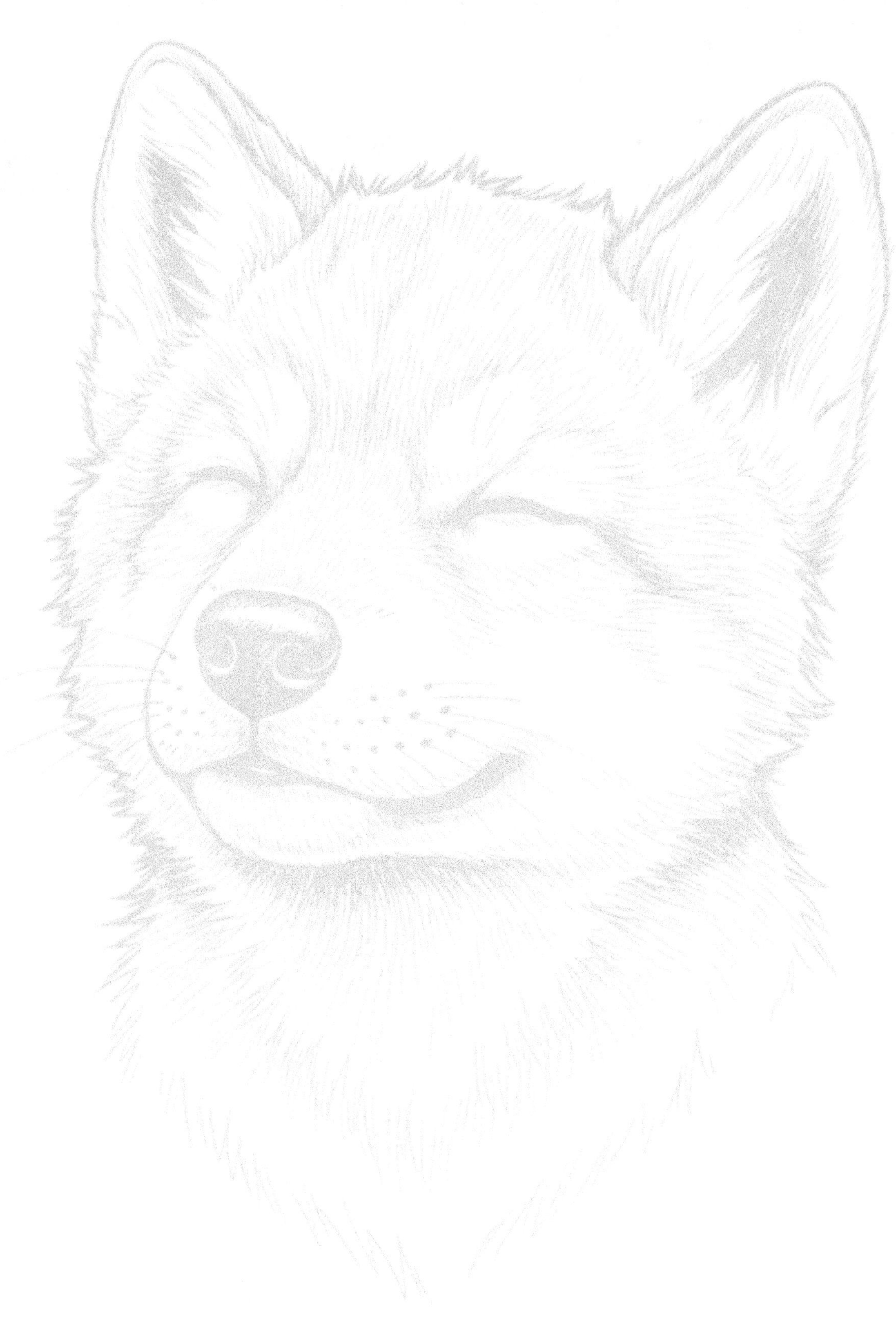

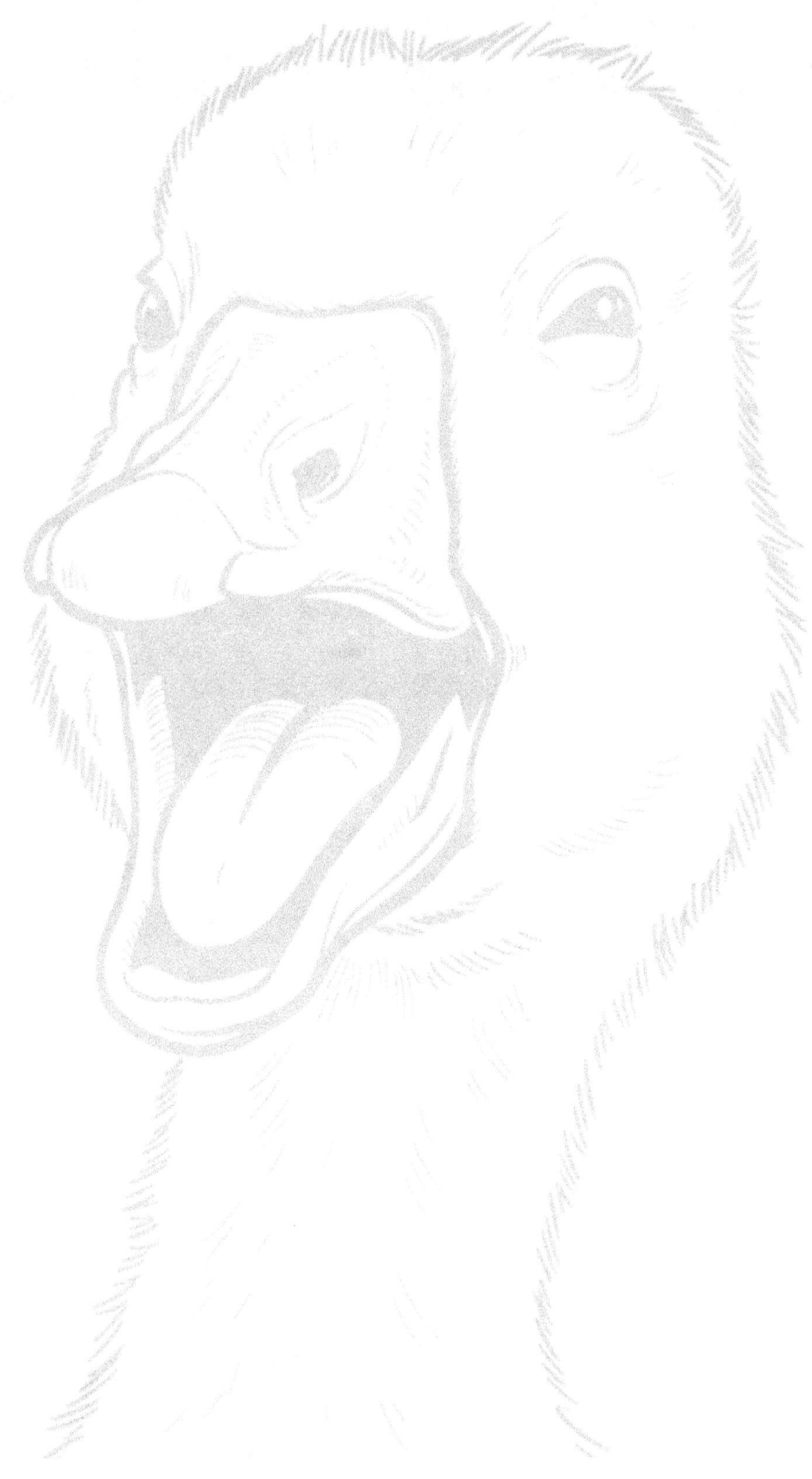

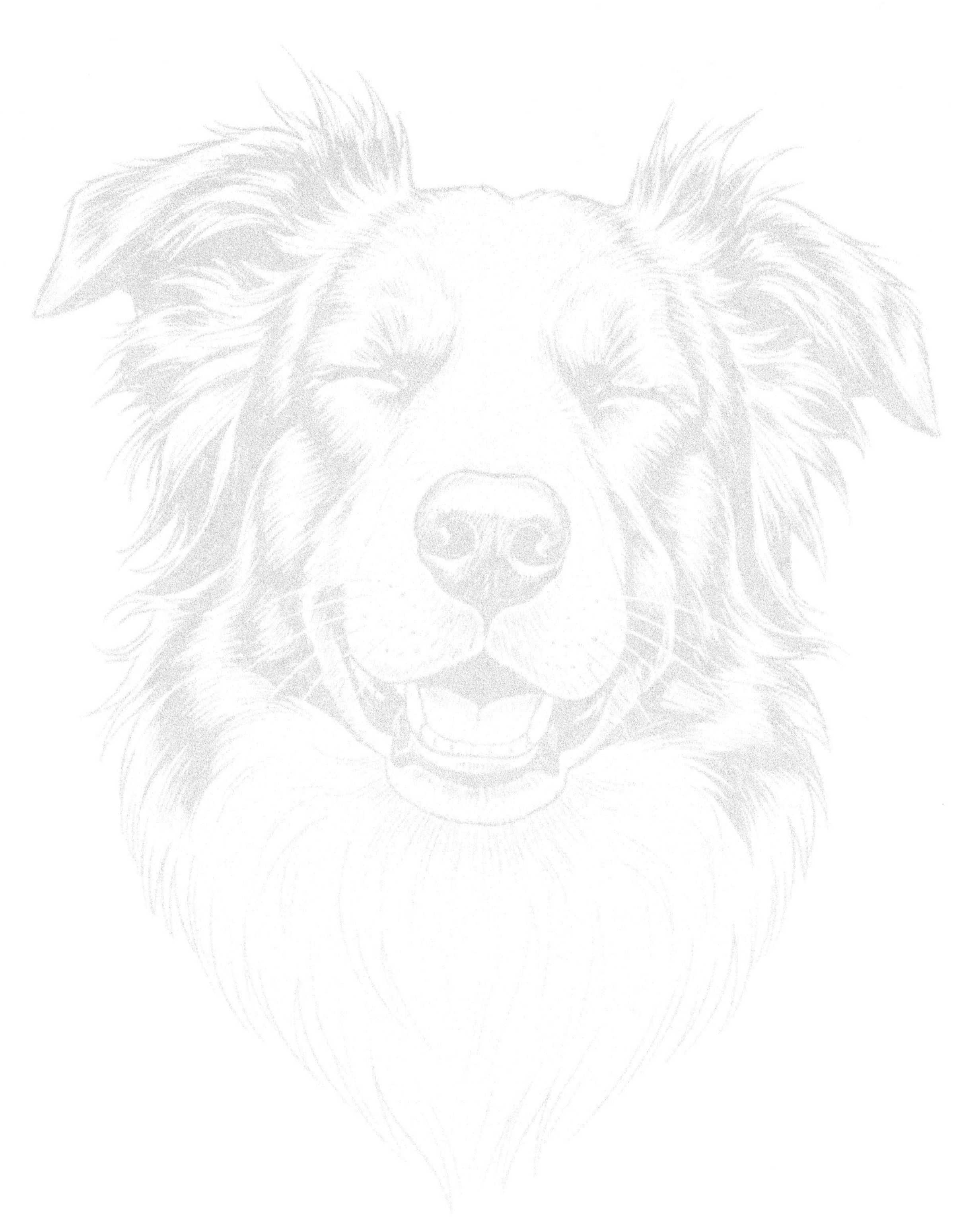

Also from Trace & Shade Studio

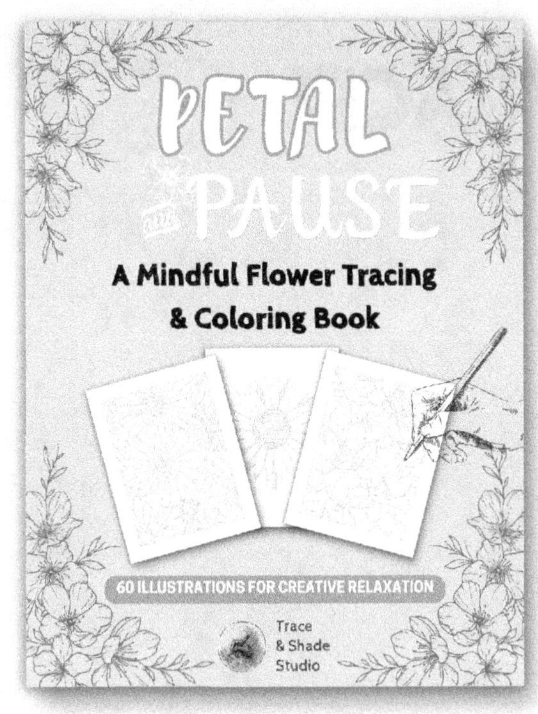

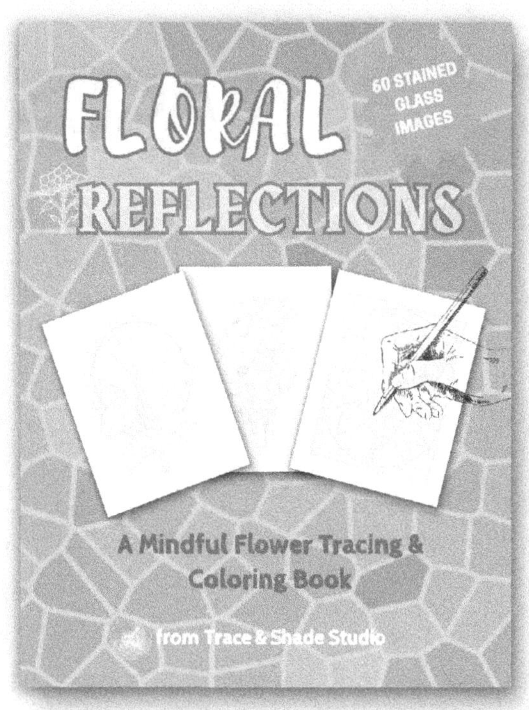

TRACE, COLOR AND RELAX MINDFULLY BY FOLLOWING BEAUTIFUL FLORAL FORMS

Available @ Amazon now here:

Available @ Amazon now here:

Get 10 MORE FREE downloadable CUTE ANIMAL FACES TO TRACE!

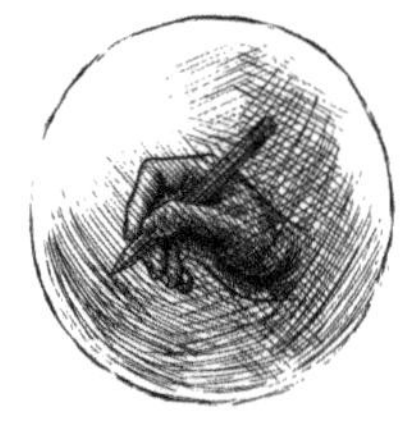

Trace & Shade Studio

www.ingramcontent.com/pod-product-compliance
Lightning Source LLC
LaVergne TN
LVHW061250100826
845148LV00008B/1082

* 9 7 9 8 8 9 9 6 8 0 6 7 0 *